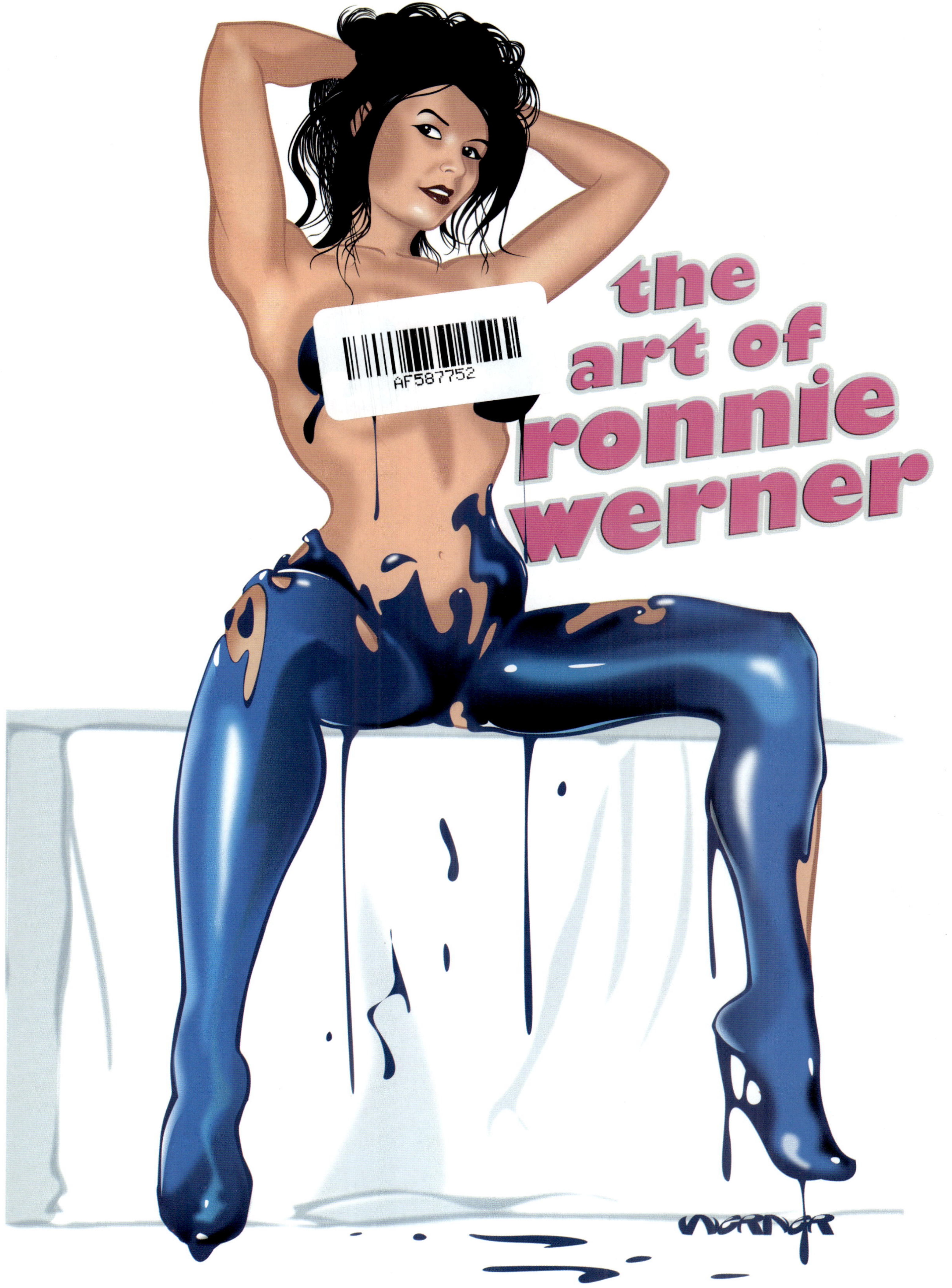

AN SQP PRESENTATION

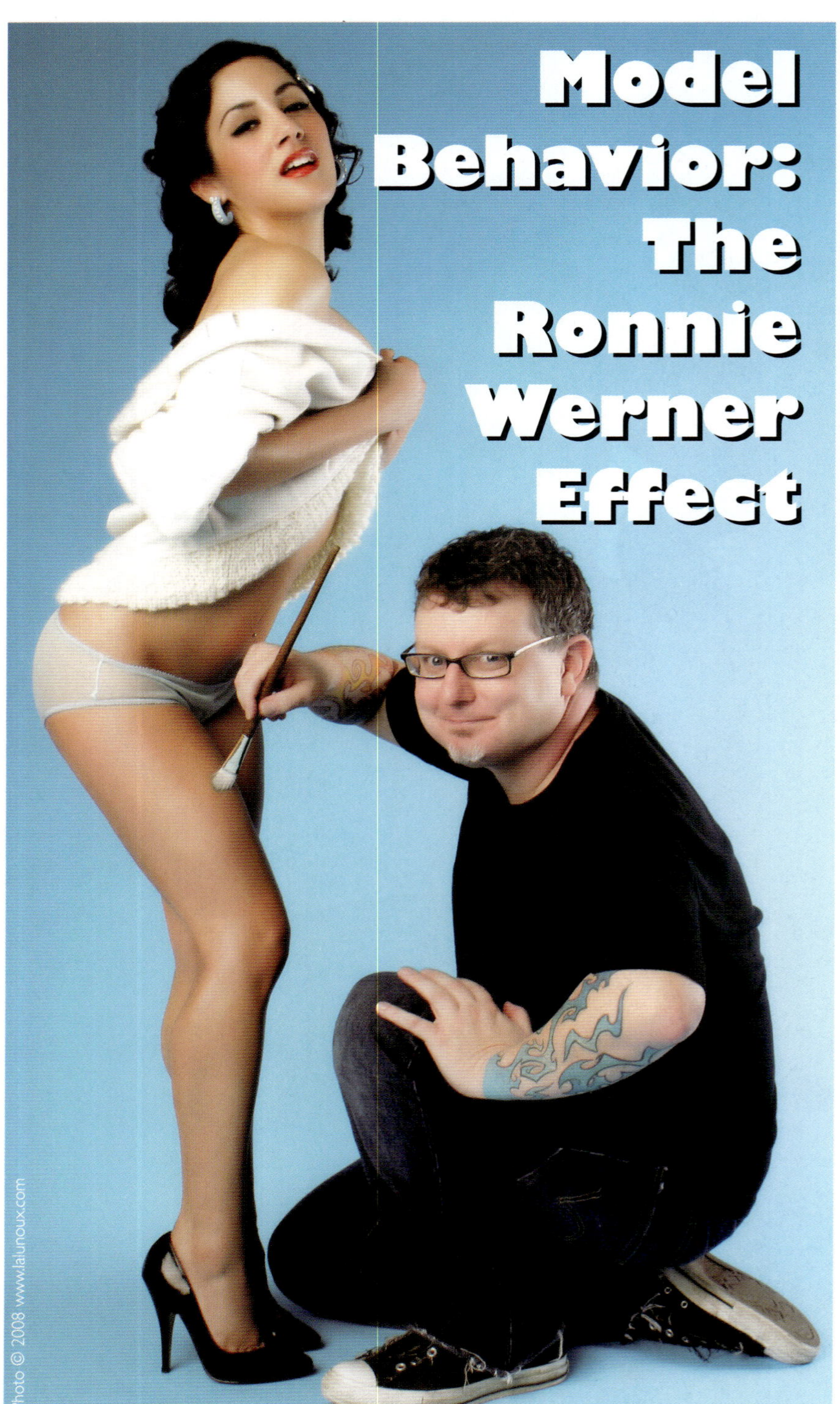

Hi, My name is Ronnie and I draw pictures of pretty naked women. Great gig for a nerdy kid from Wisconsin huh?

I was born in the Winter of 1965. Not long after that I started drawing. At first I copied the great comic book masters Jack Kirby, George Tuska, John Byrne and many others. Almost immediately after puberty I discovered the Playboys my dad hid under his dresser. One of the great revelations of my life was finding those amazing Vargas pin ups. I soon after discovered Petty, Elvgren, and any other pin up artist I could find. My dream of being a pin up artist was born.

I briefly attended the Art Institute of Chicago and the Pacific Northwest College of Art. There I toyed with the idea of becoming a "legitimate" artist. In the end I returned to my first loves, comics and naked women.

A little about my process: I use models in most of my work, wonderful, beautiful models. I draw the pin ups using pencil and paper and then scan the drawing on to my Mac. do all the color work in Adobe Illustrator.

If you would like to drop me a line I'd love to hear from you. ronnie@ronniewerner.com

Best,
Ronnie Werner
September, 2008

Ronnie would like to thank the following people for their inspiration, kindness and help along the way.
Kevin Eastman, Ken Keirns, Malachi Maloney, Chris Cunico, Greg Glover, Billy Hofmeister, Pete and Lisa Strolis, Doug Siglin, Sarah Wilson, Harper, Ellen and Marc, Karyn and Johnny Servin, Mom, Dad, and Bunner.

All the beautiful and amazing models I have had the pleasure of working with.

A special thanks to Veronika Kotlajic who has been a perfect muse, but more importantly, an incredible friend.

The Art of Ronnie Werner Volume 1

Book design by Grassy Knoll Studios.

Published by
SQP Inc.
PO Box 248 - Columbus, NJ 08022

Sal Quartuccio & Bob Keenan - Publishers

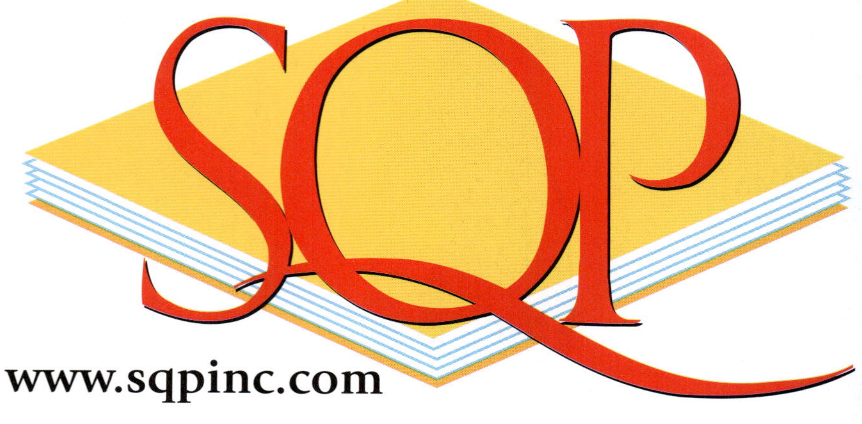

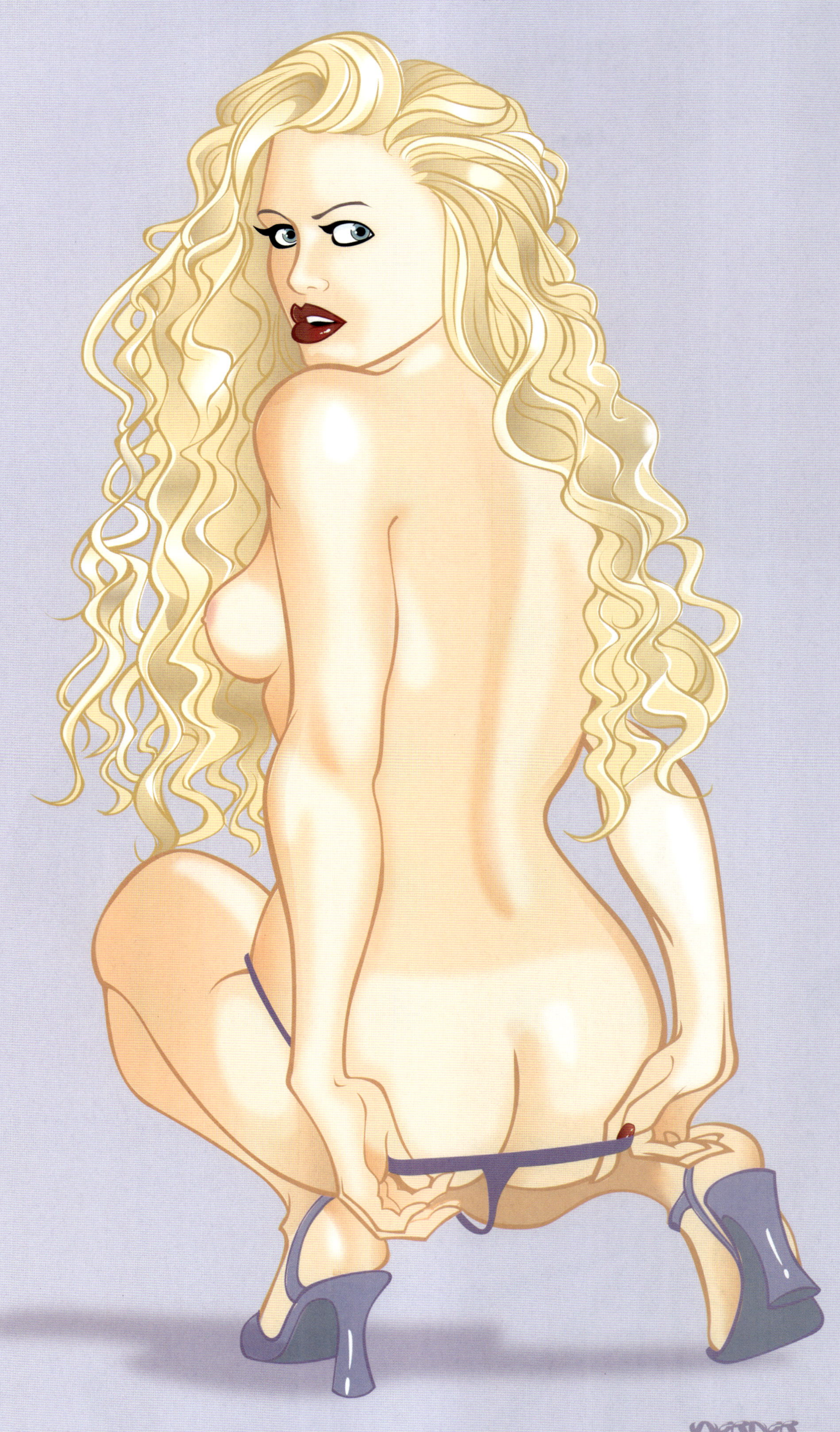

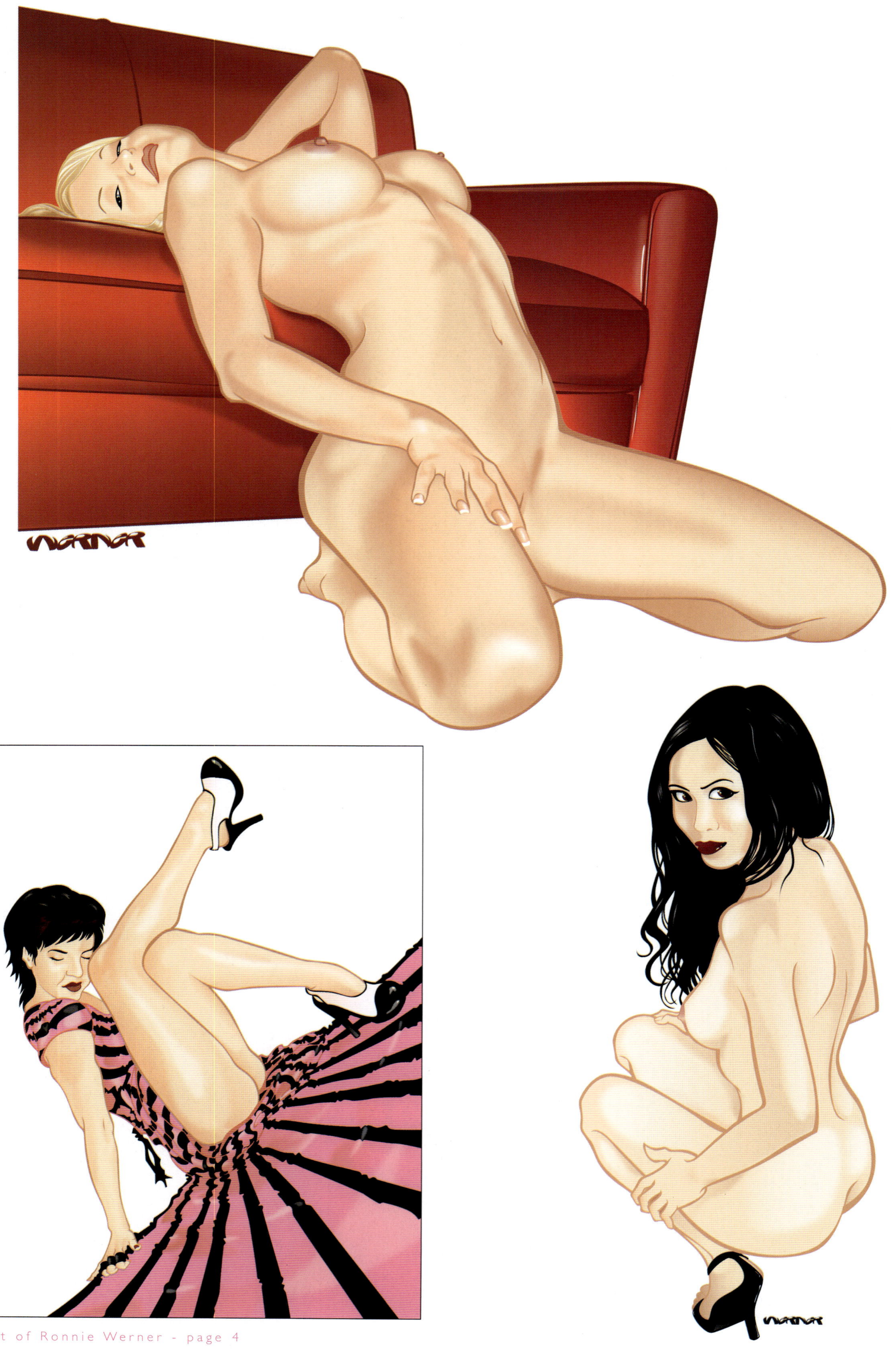
WERNER
WERNER

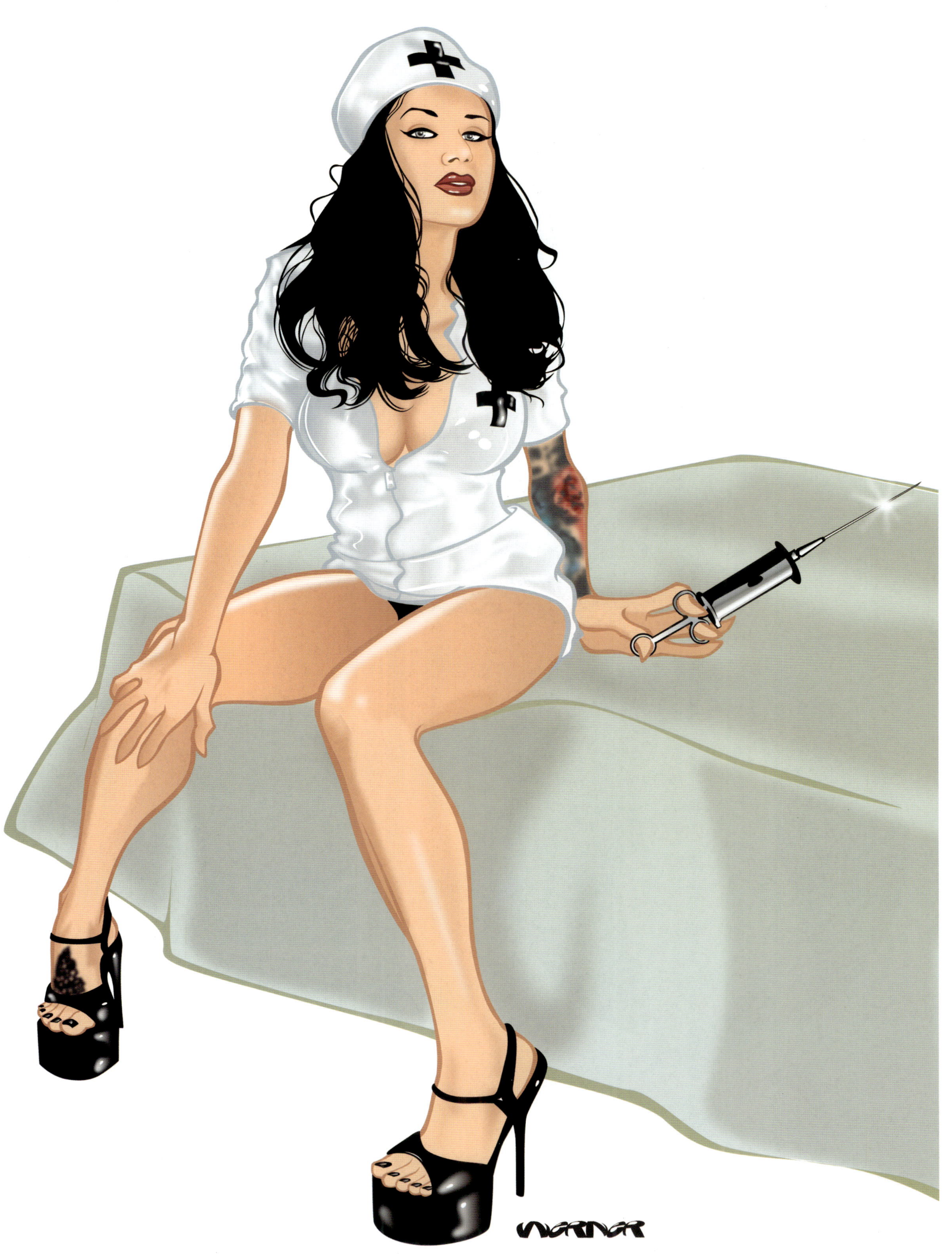
WERNER

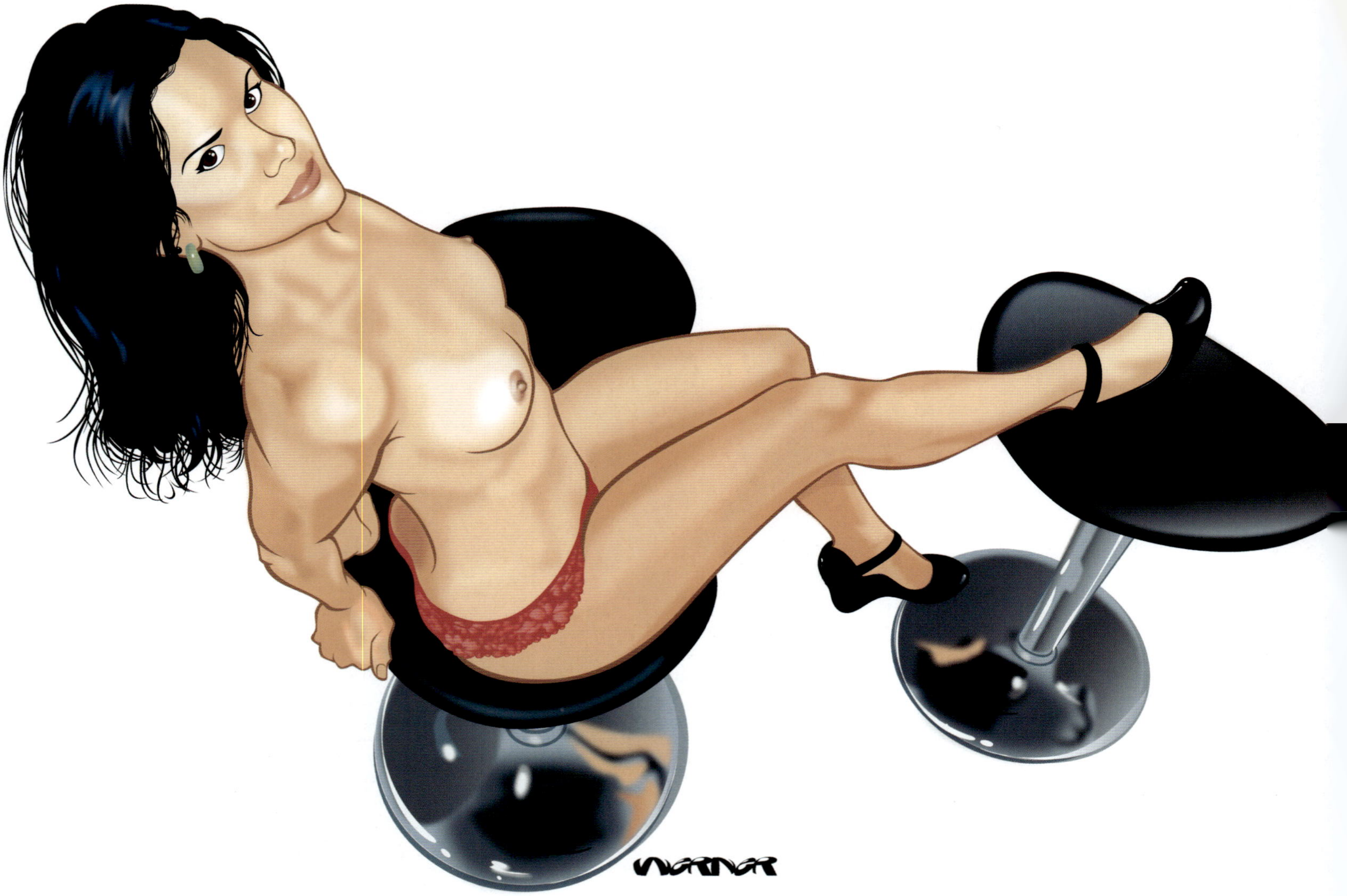

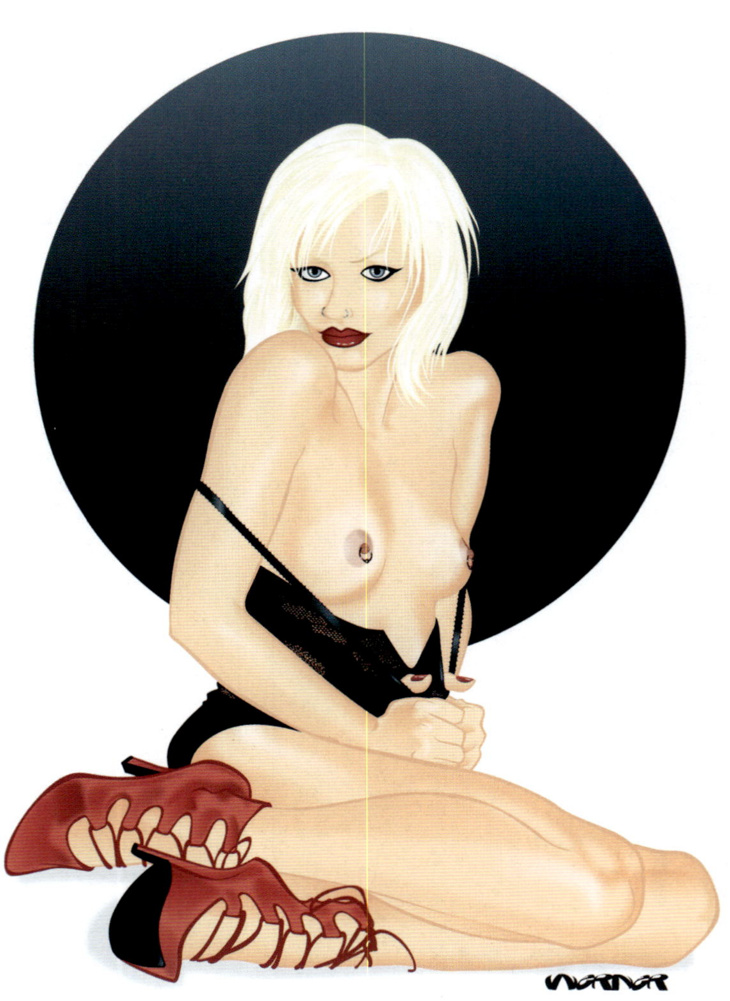

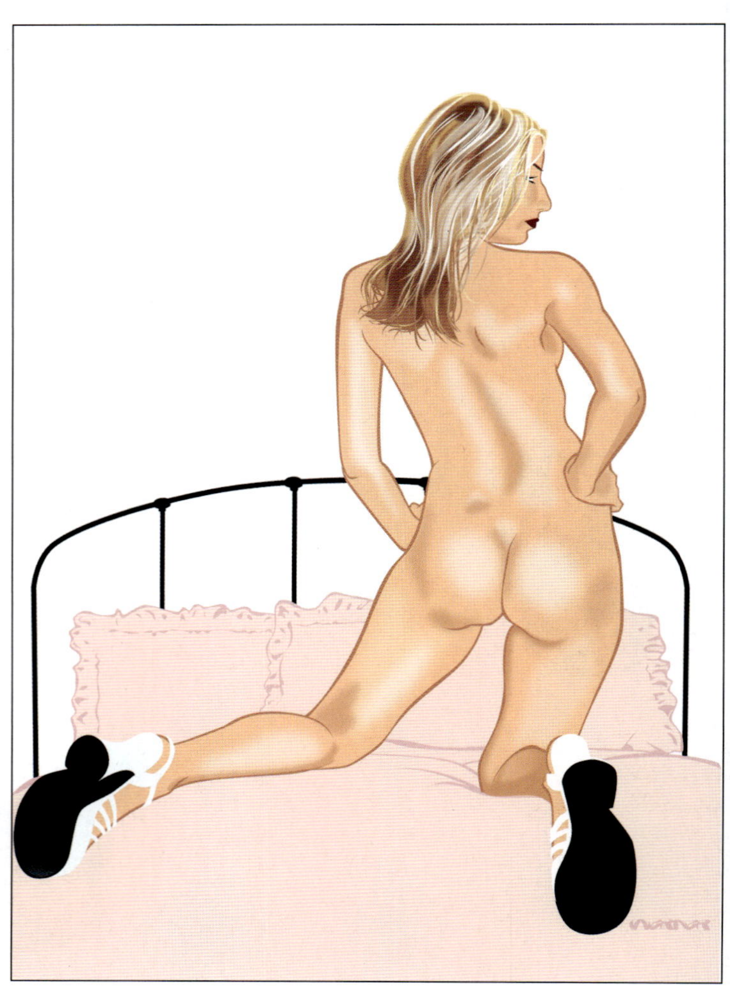

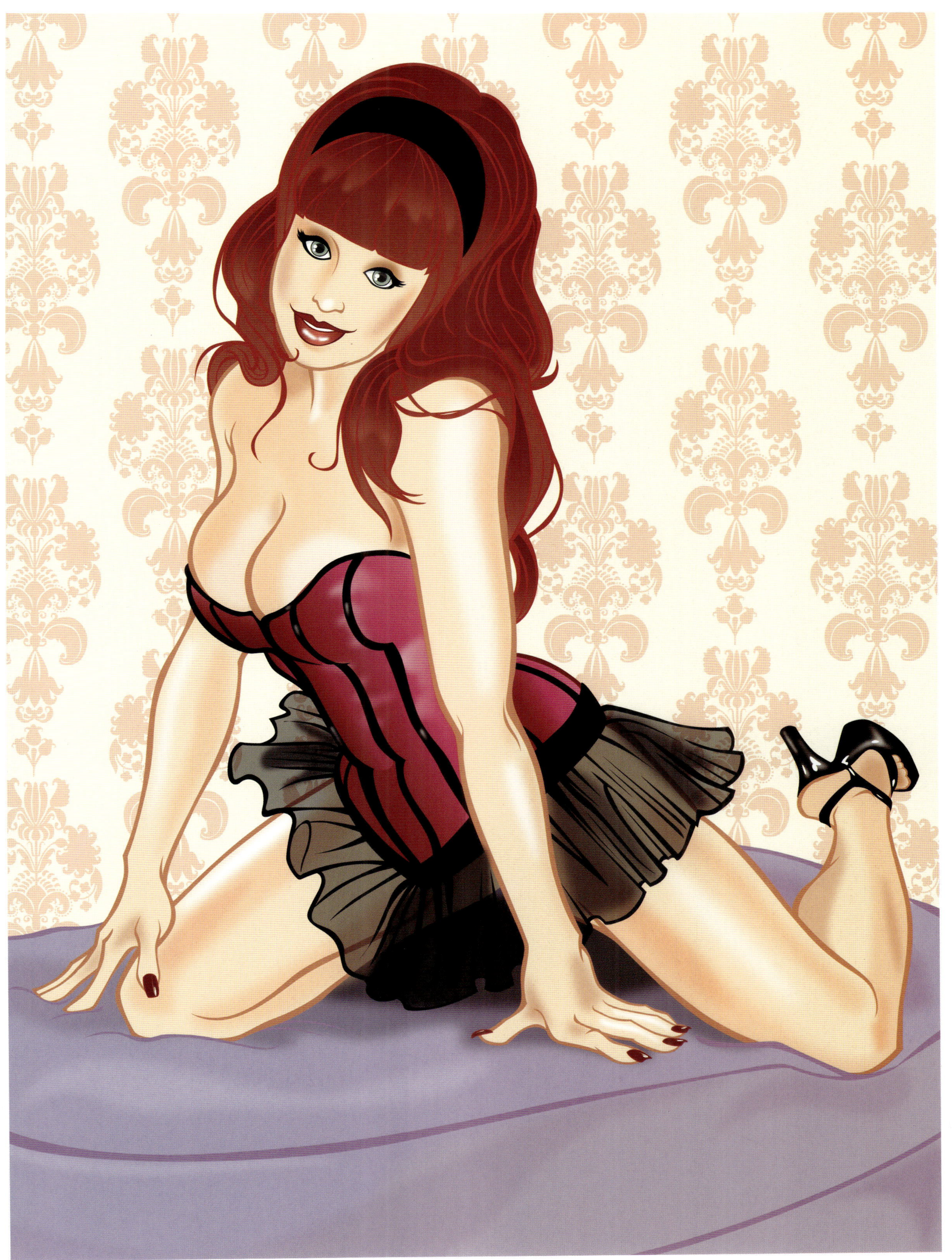

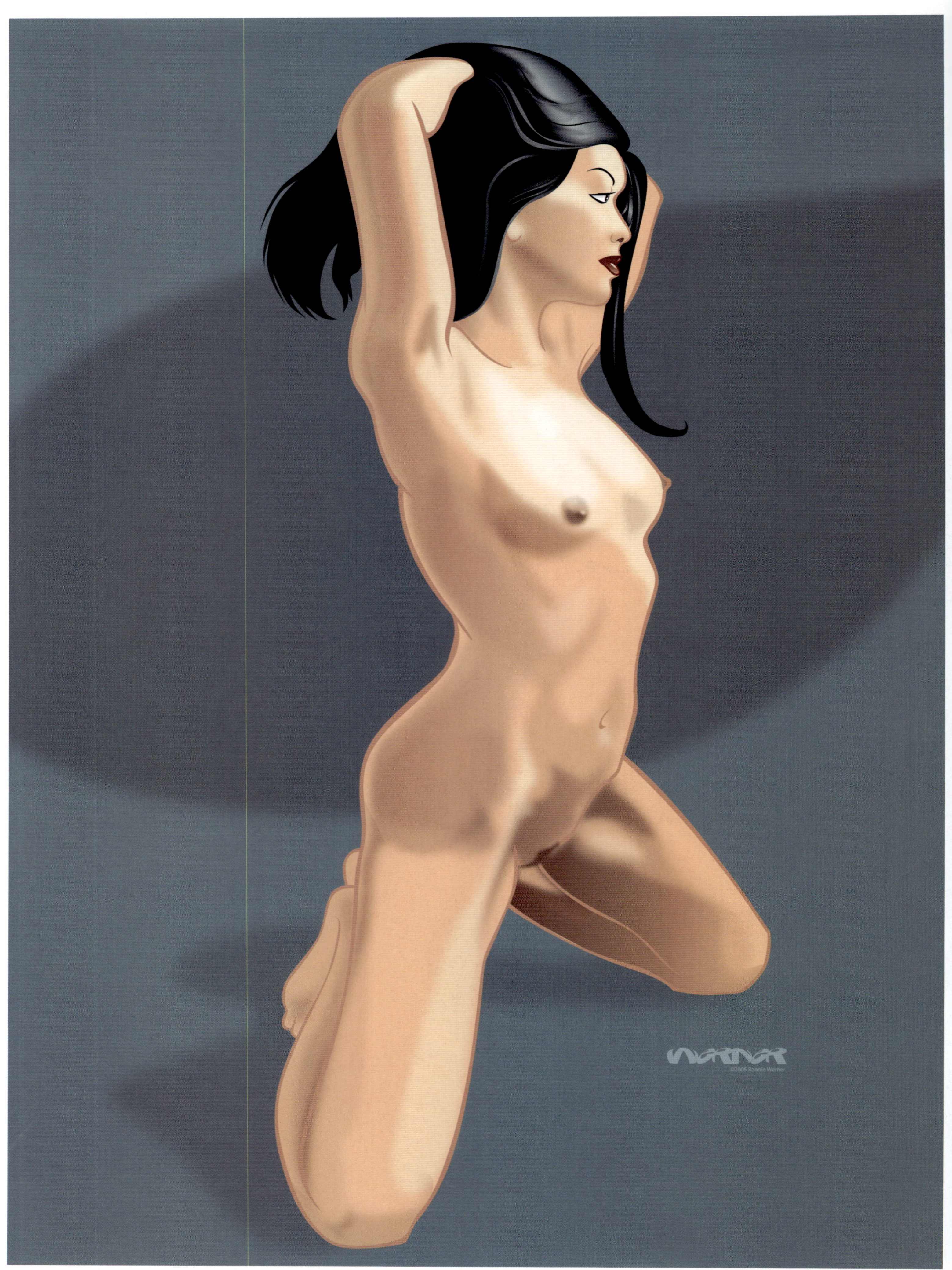
WERNER
©2005 Ronnie Werner

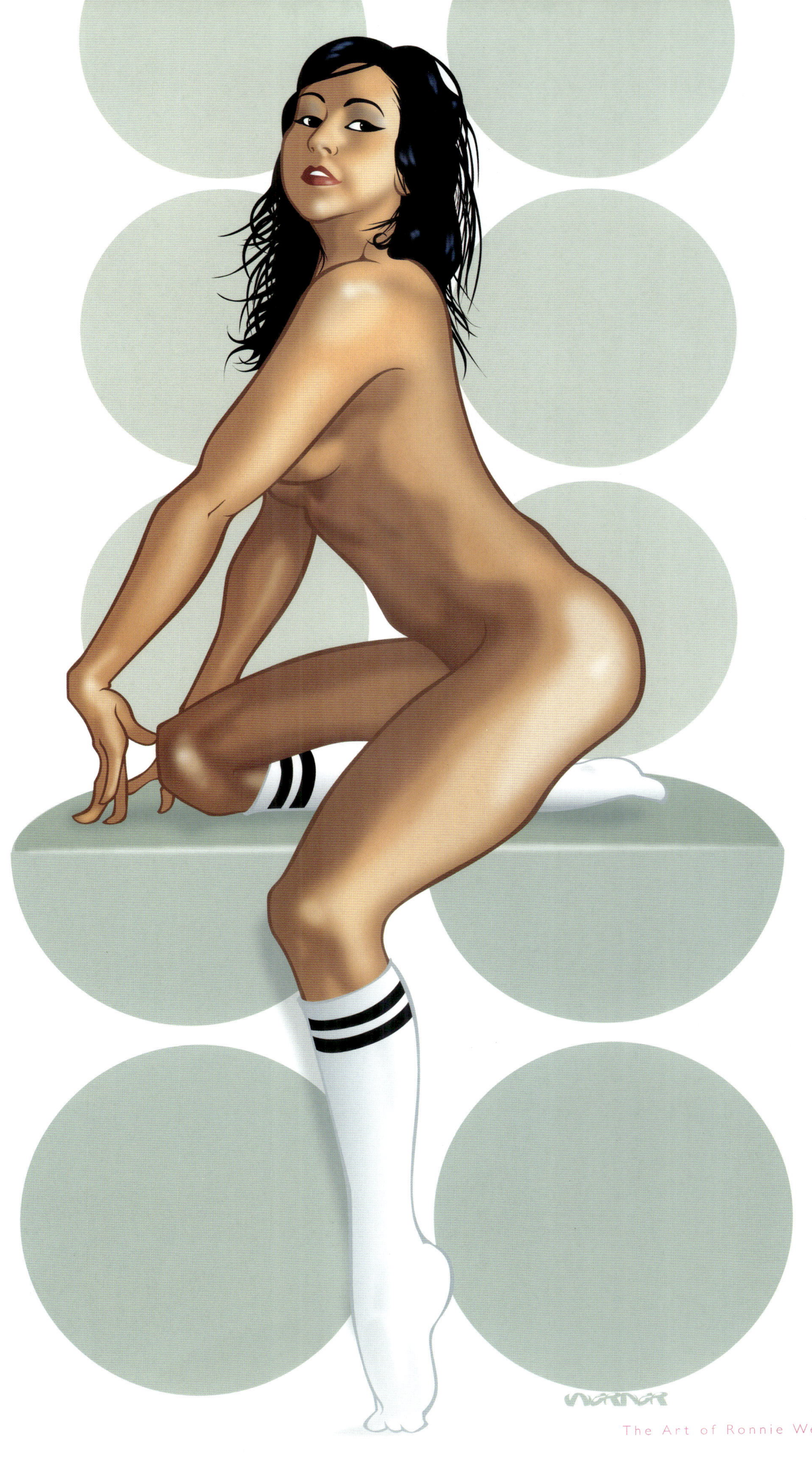

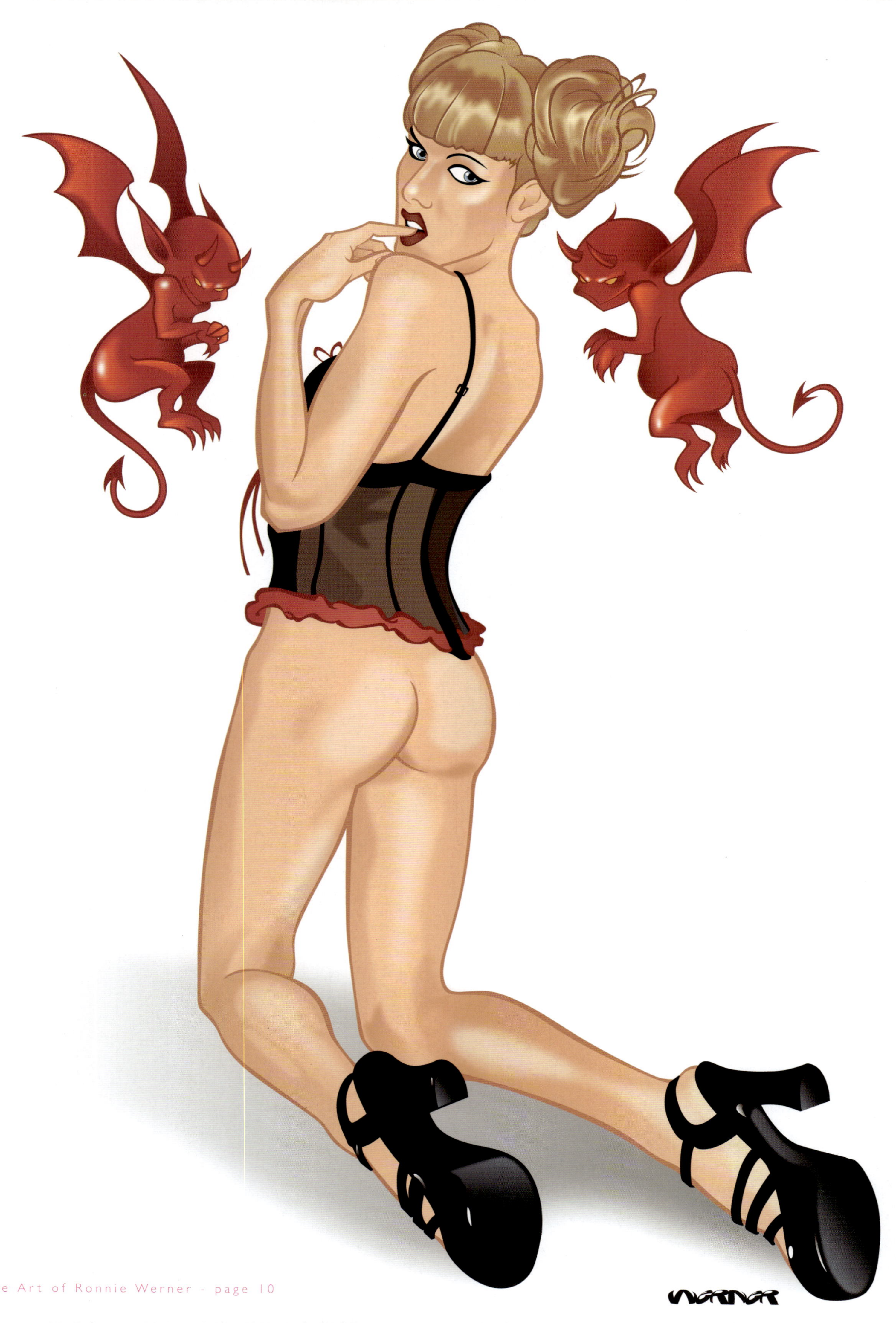
Werner

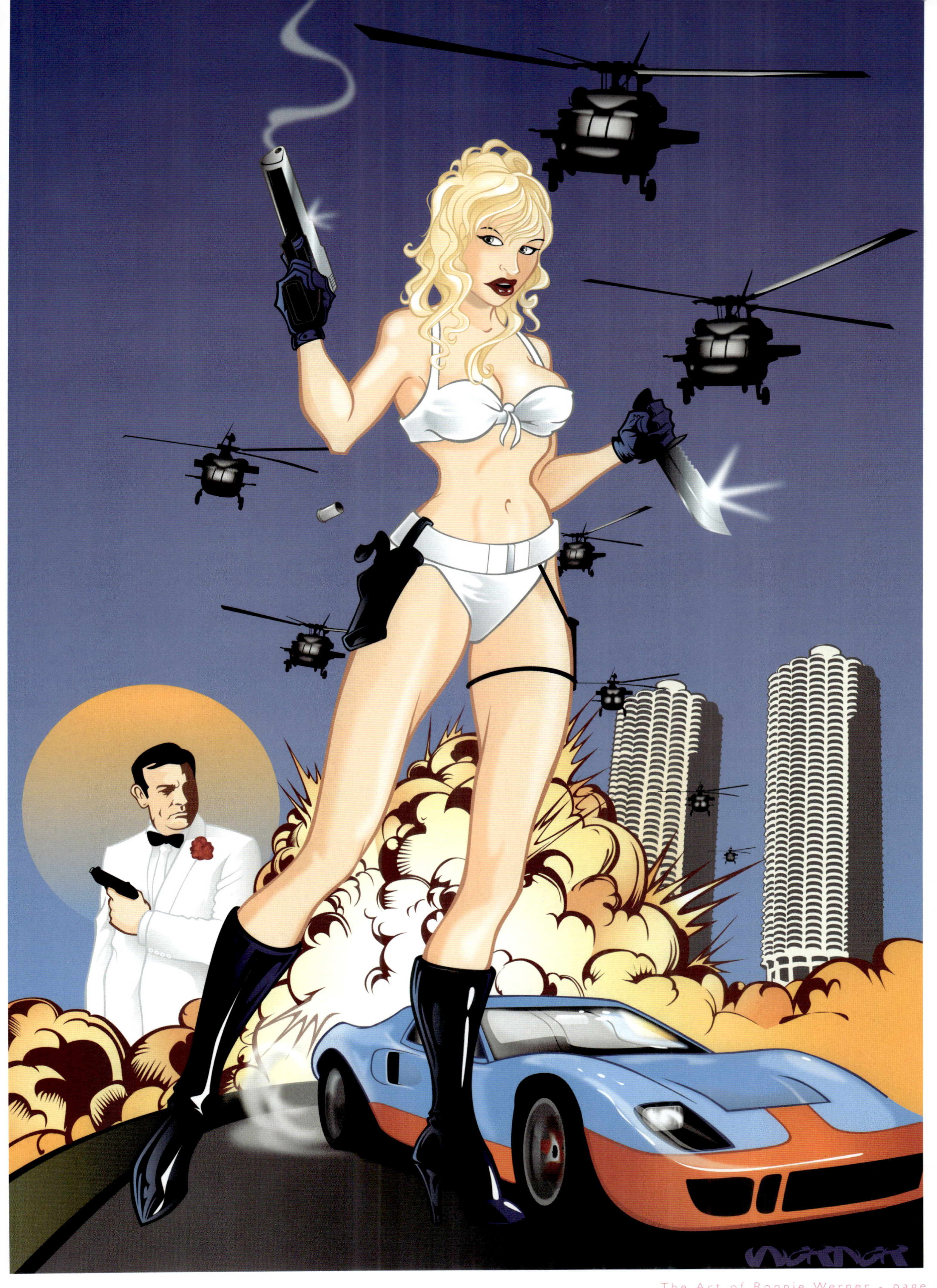
Werner

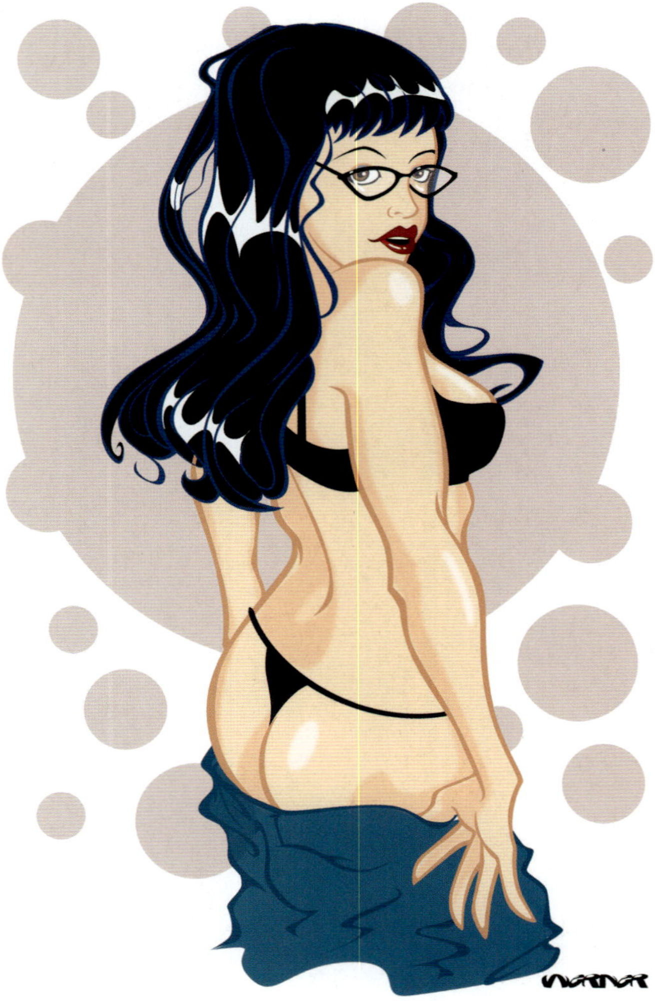

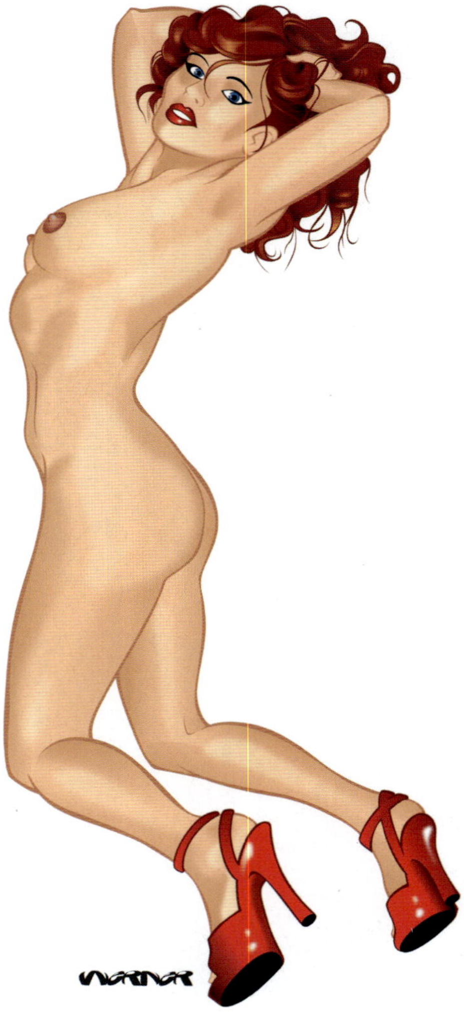

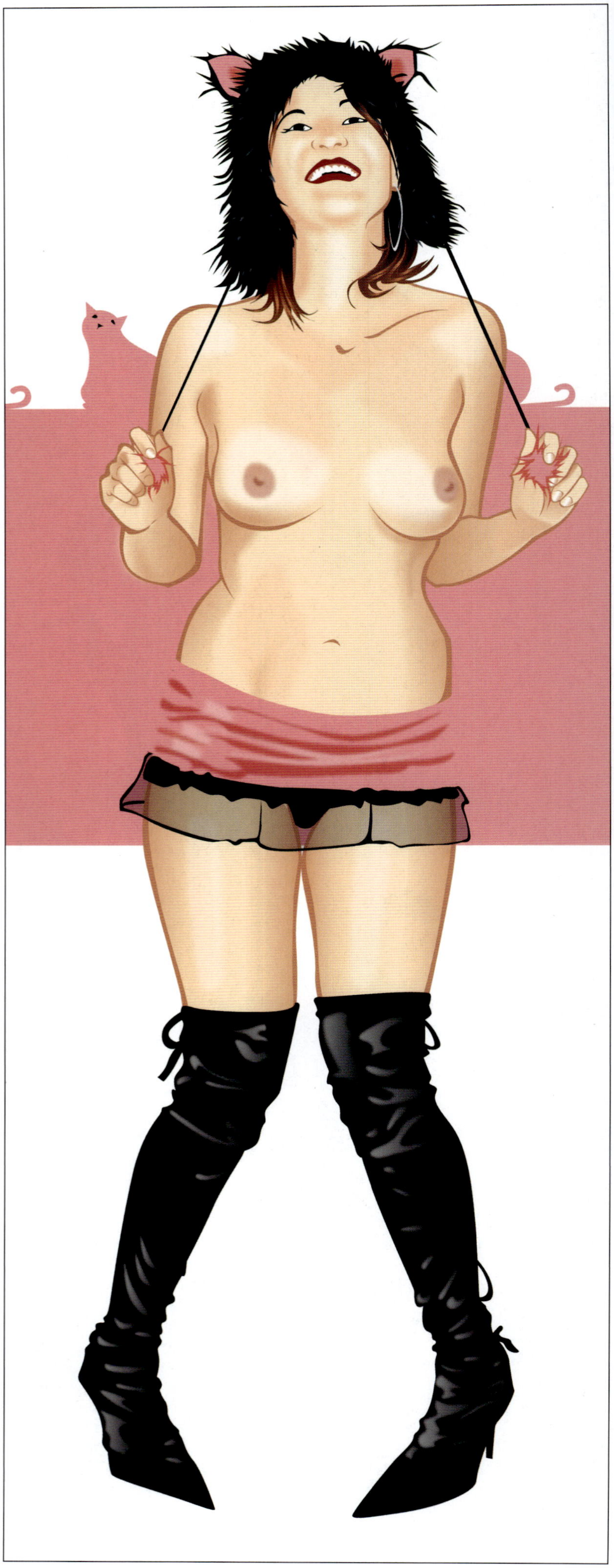

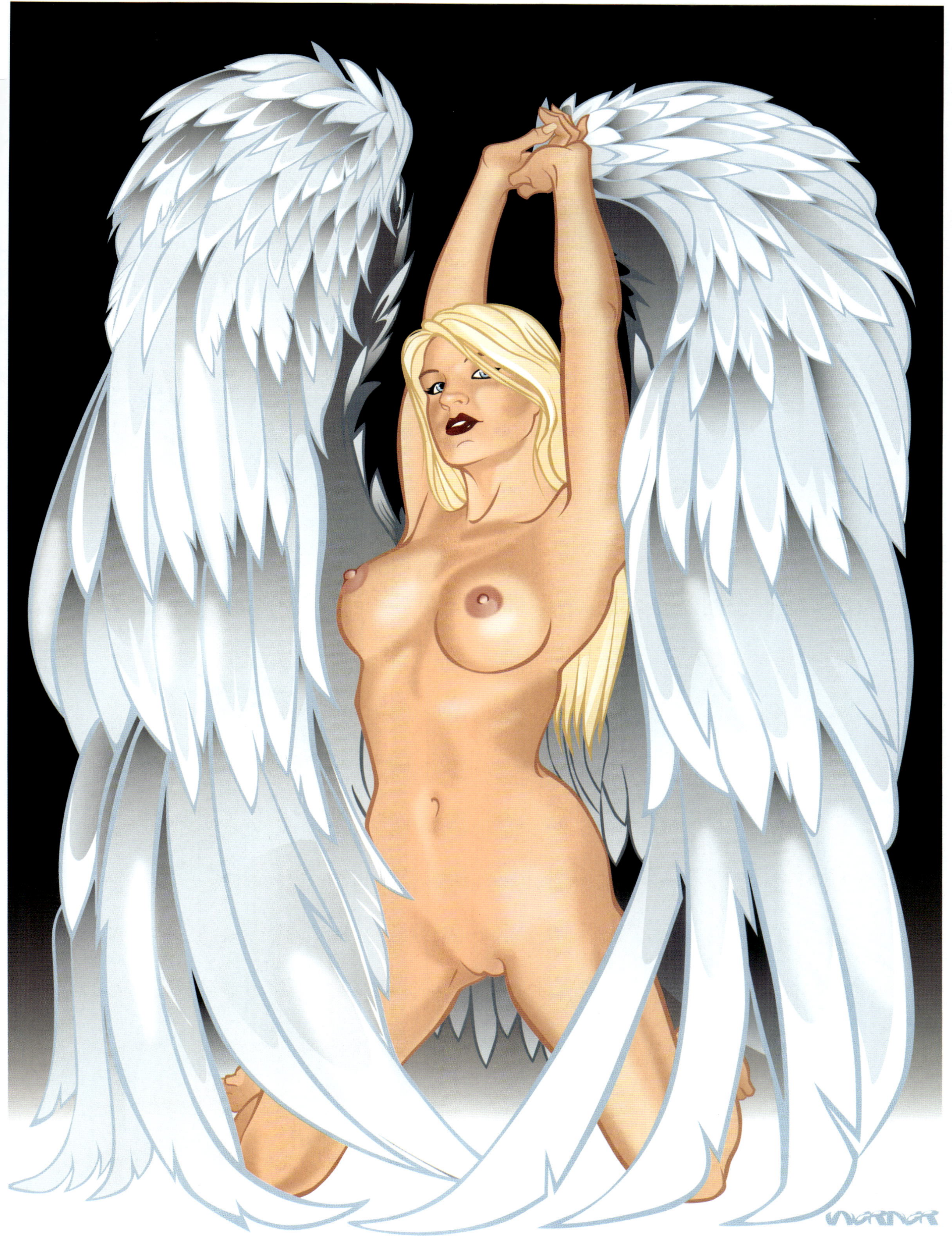
Werner

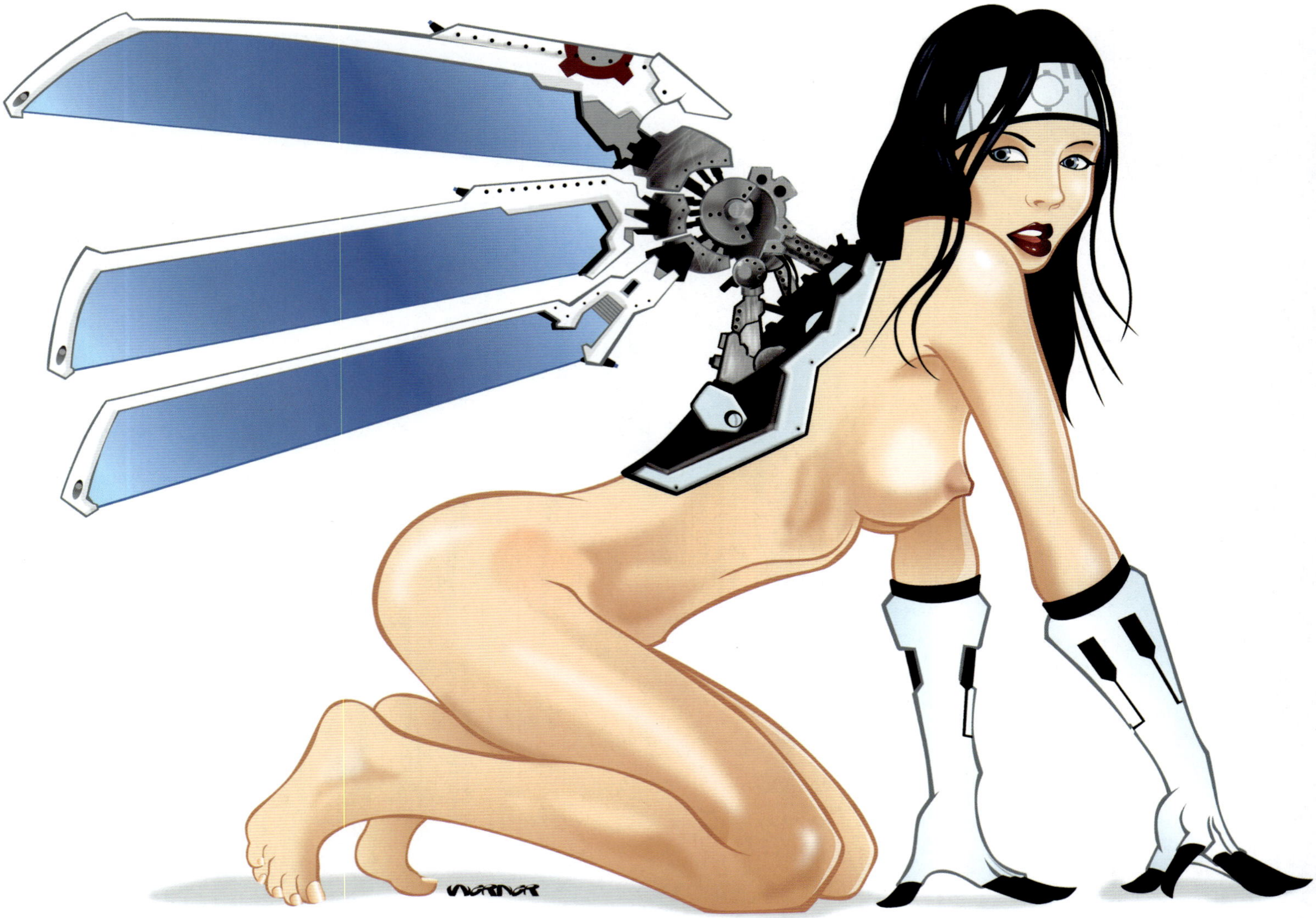

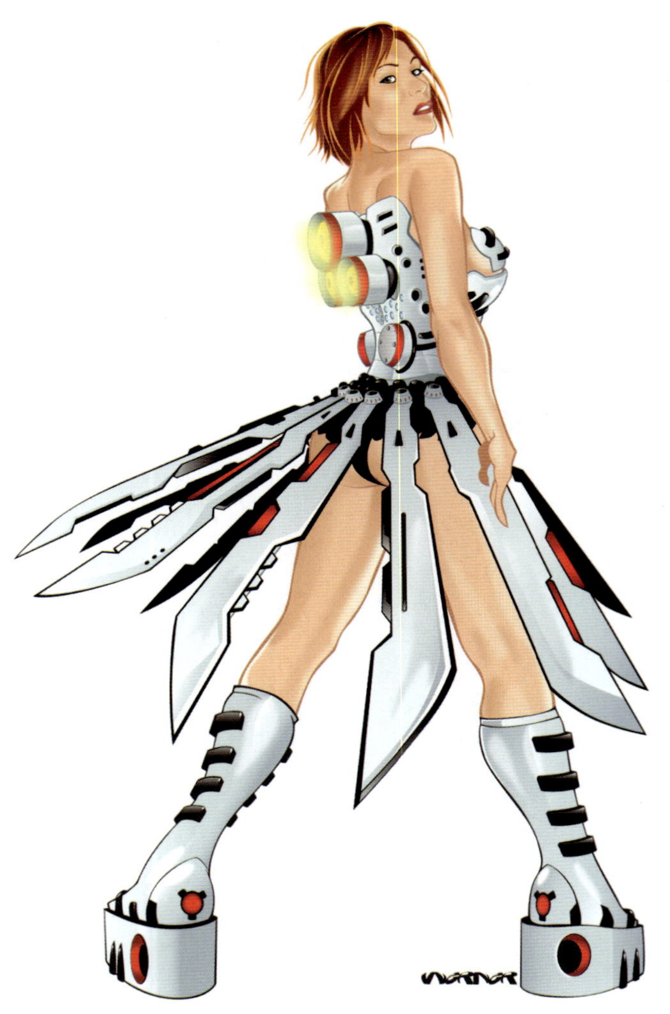

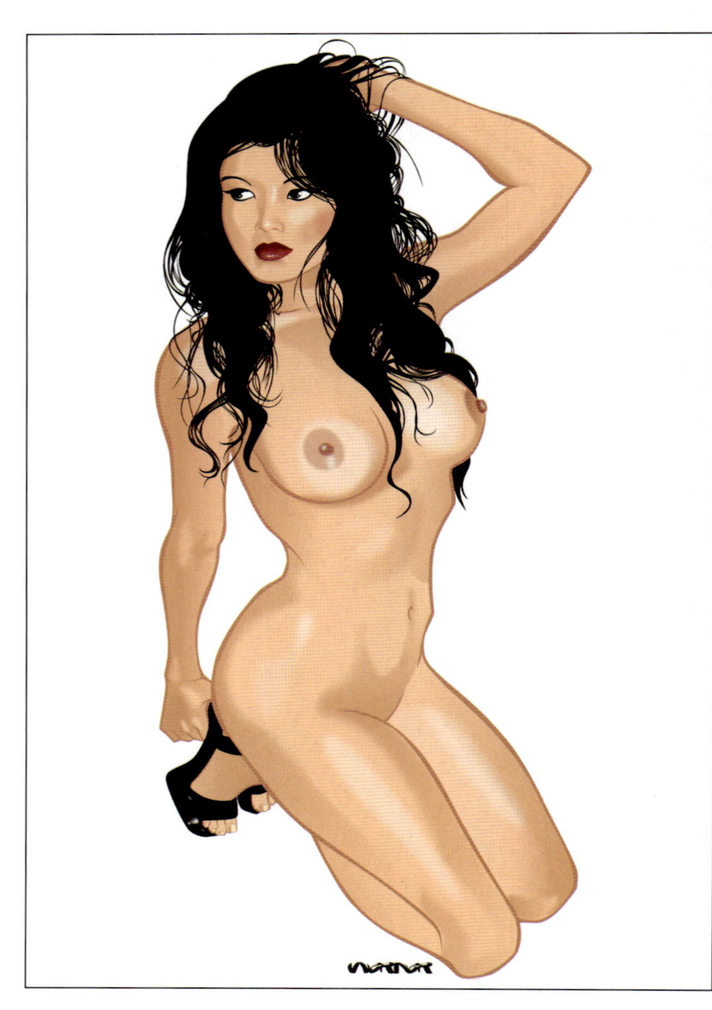

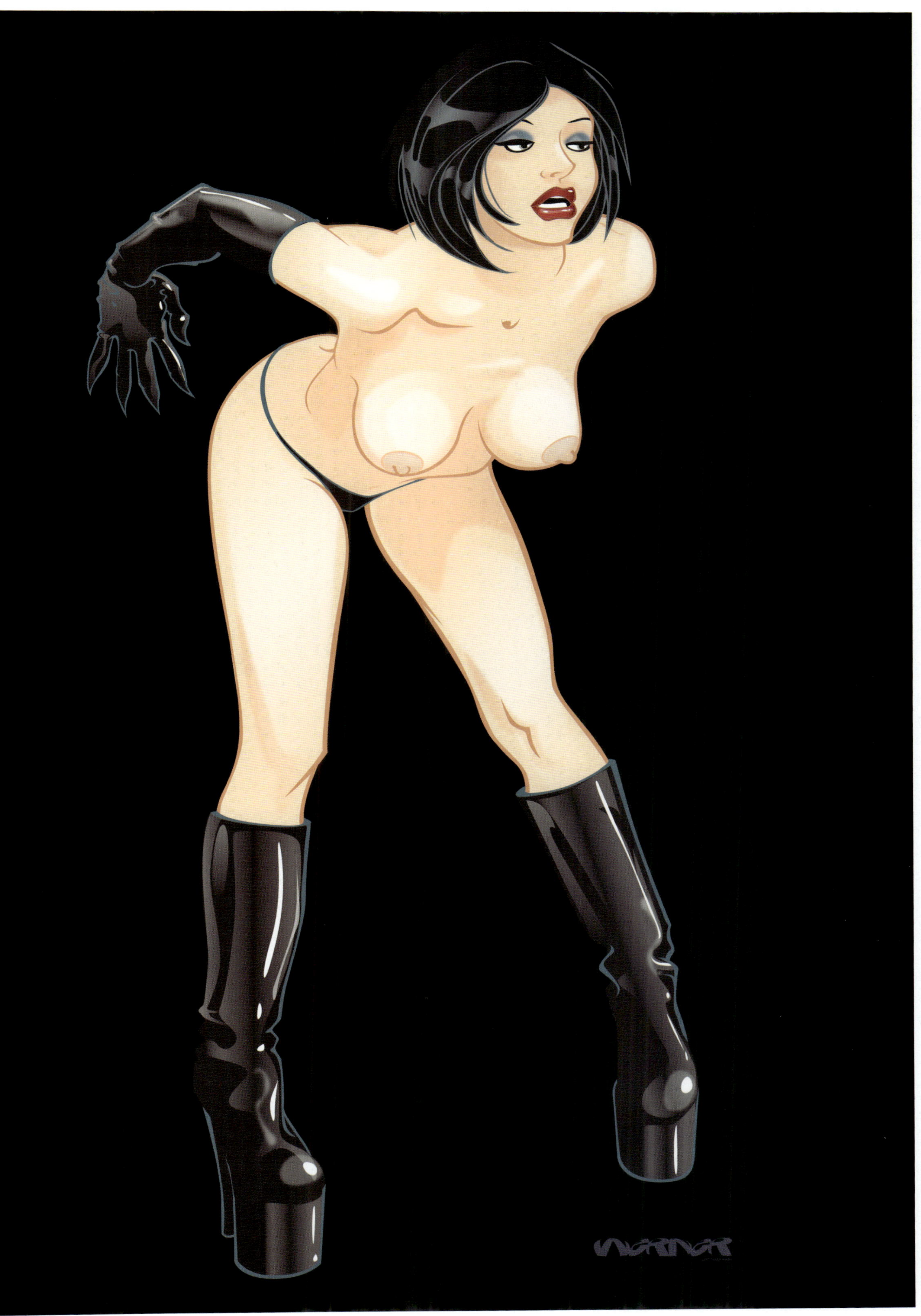

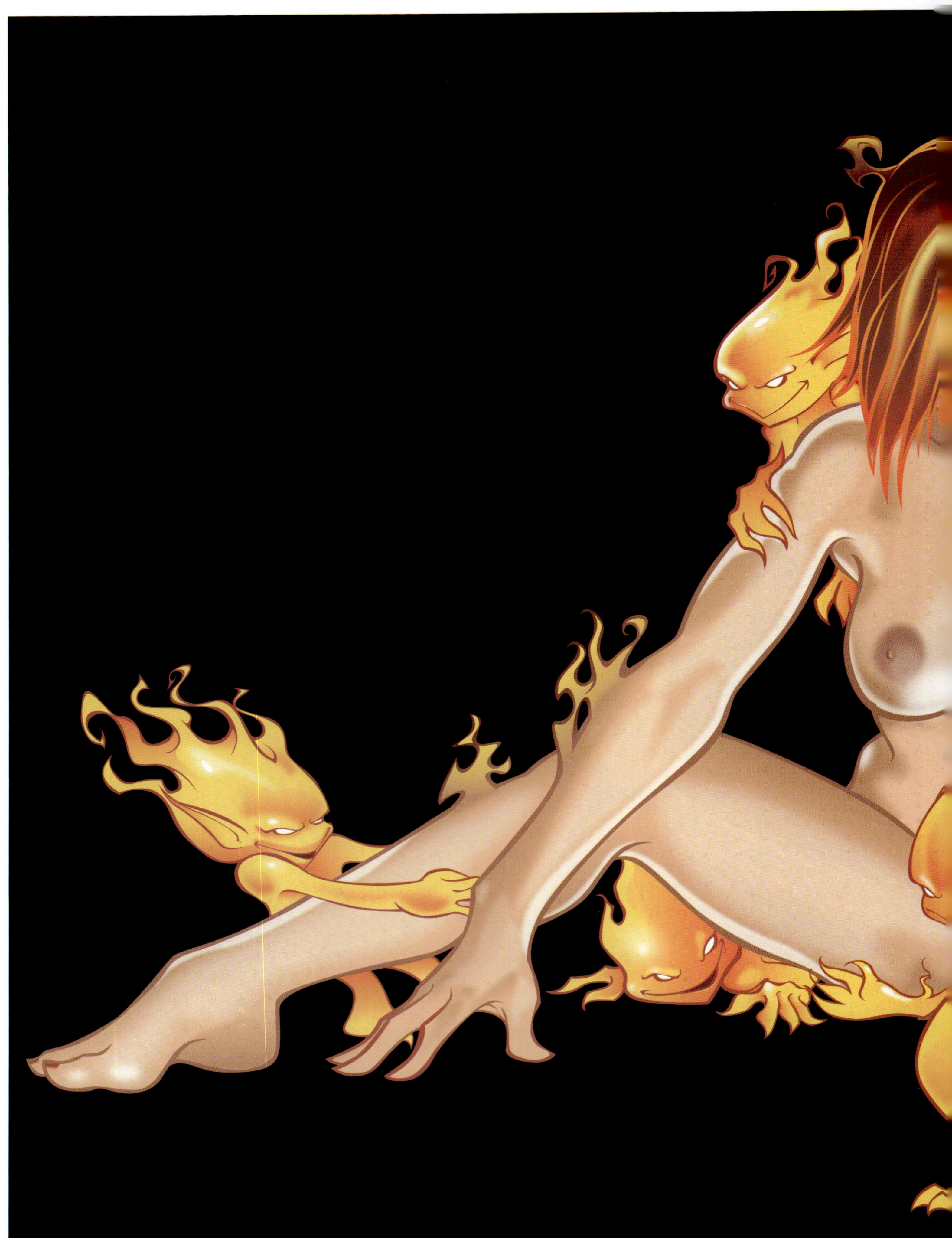

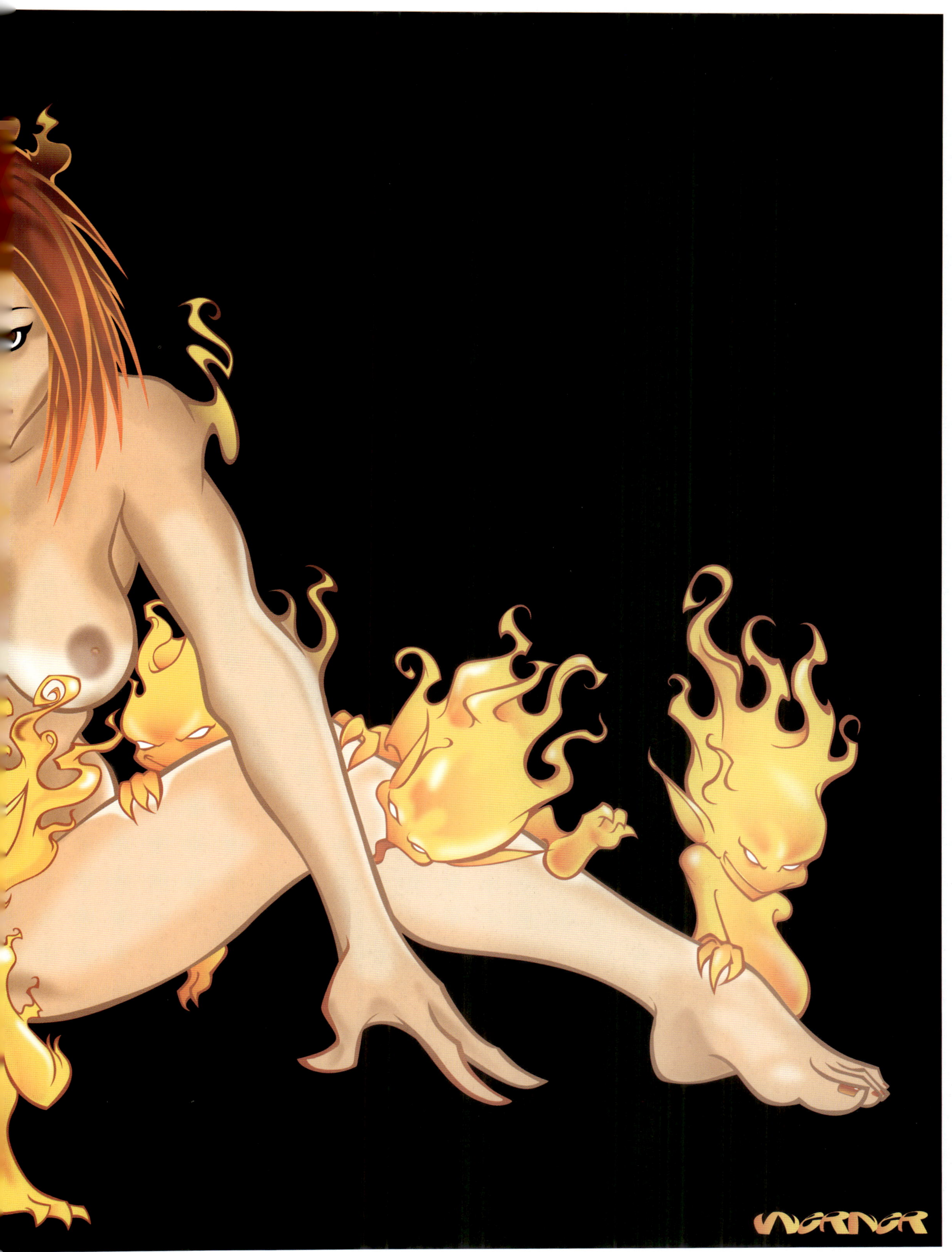
WERNER

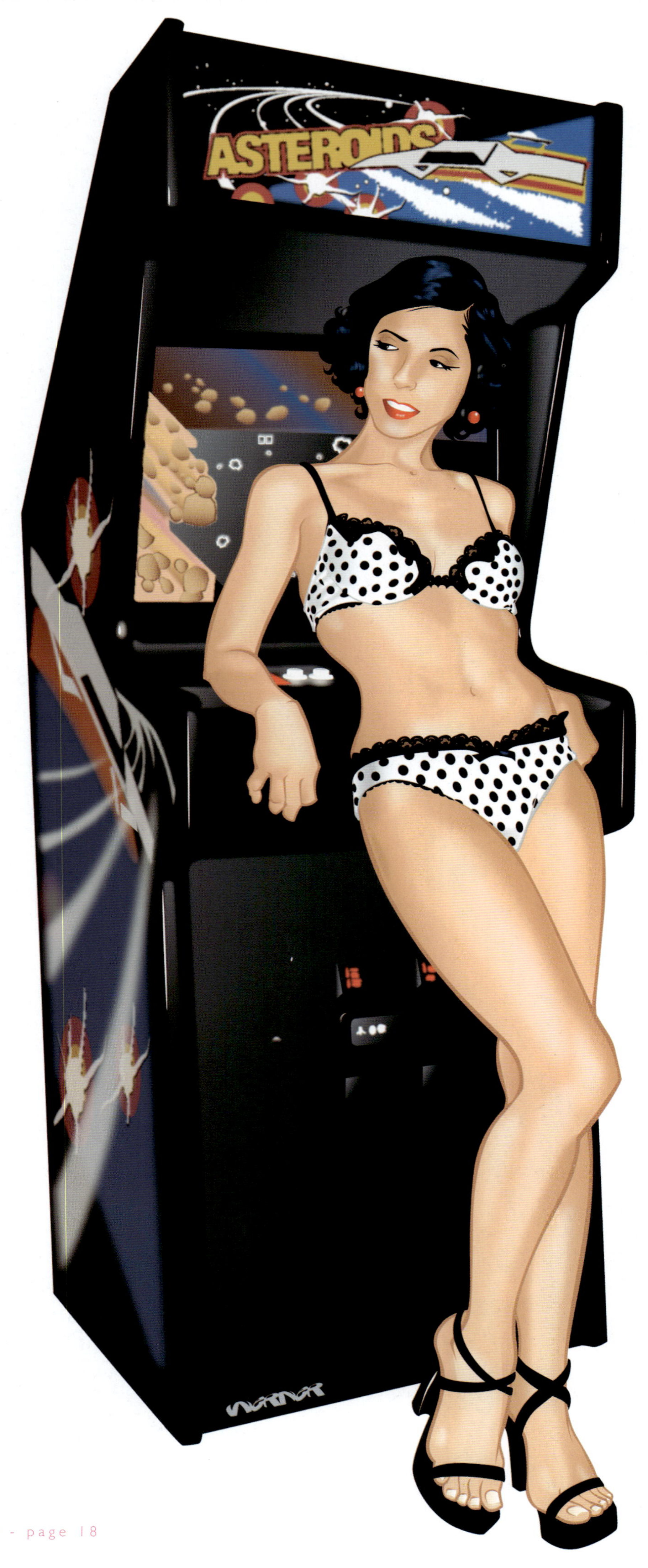
ASTEROIDS
werner

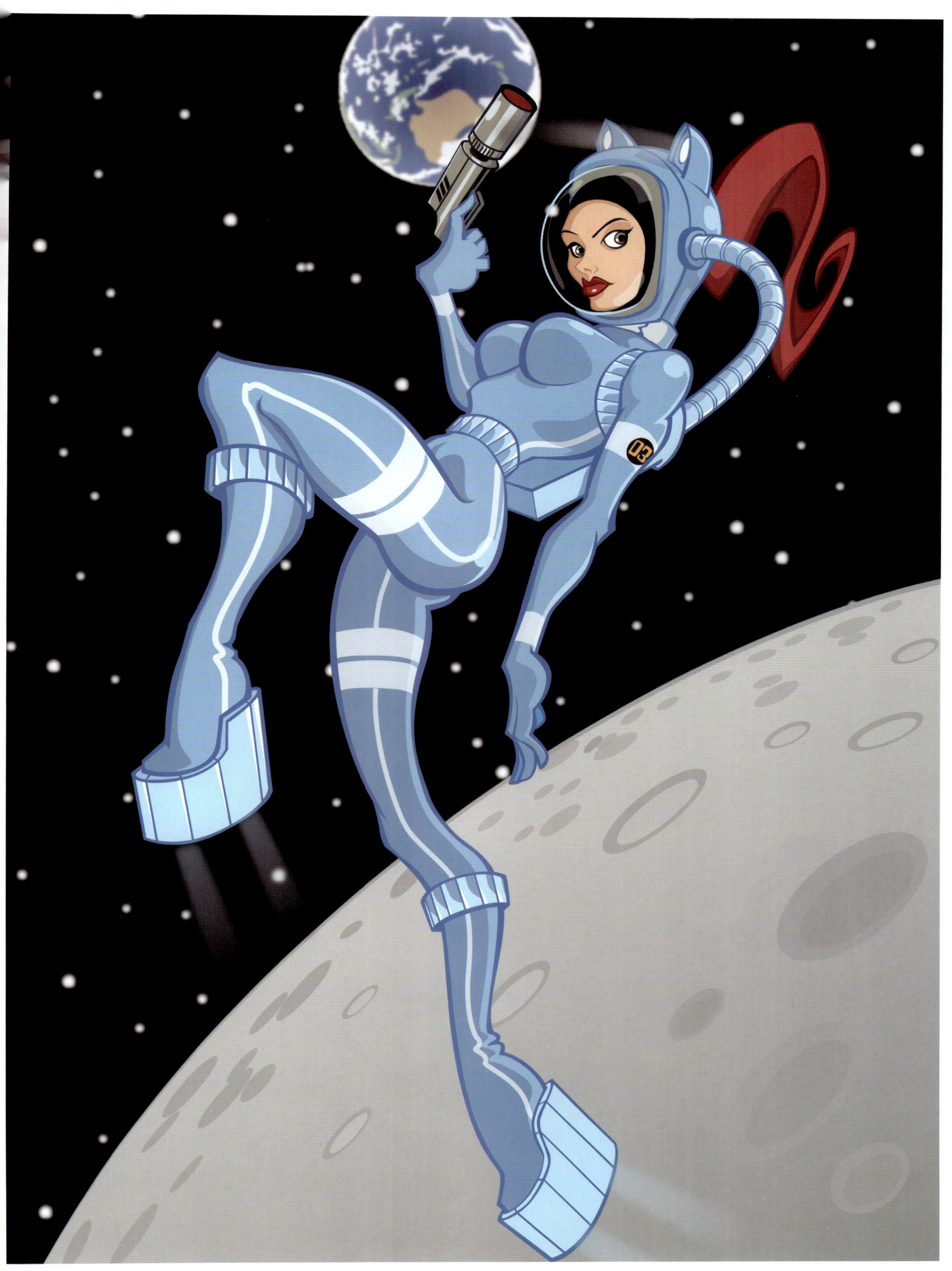
03

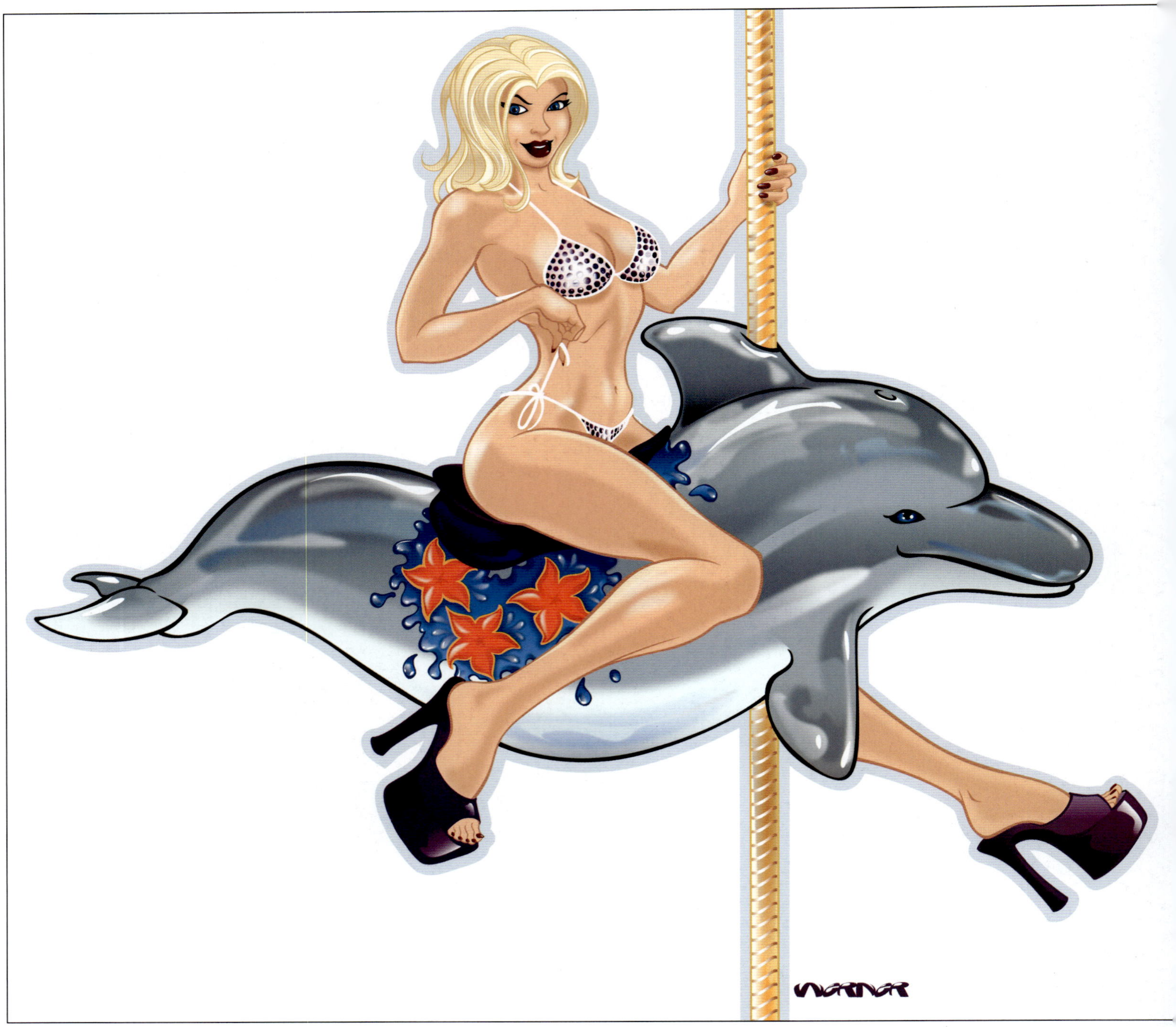

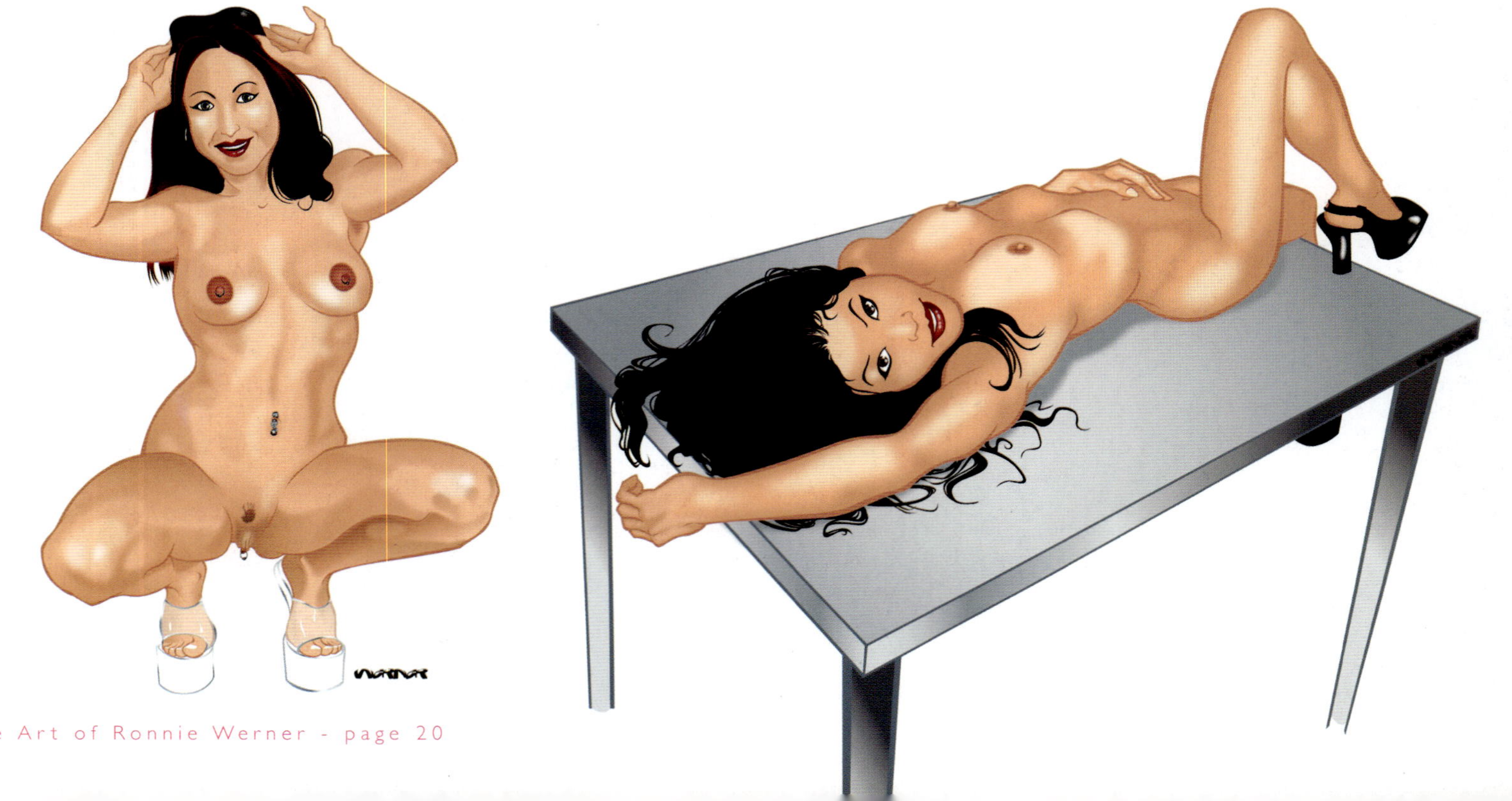

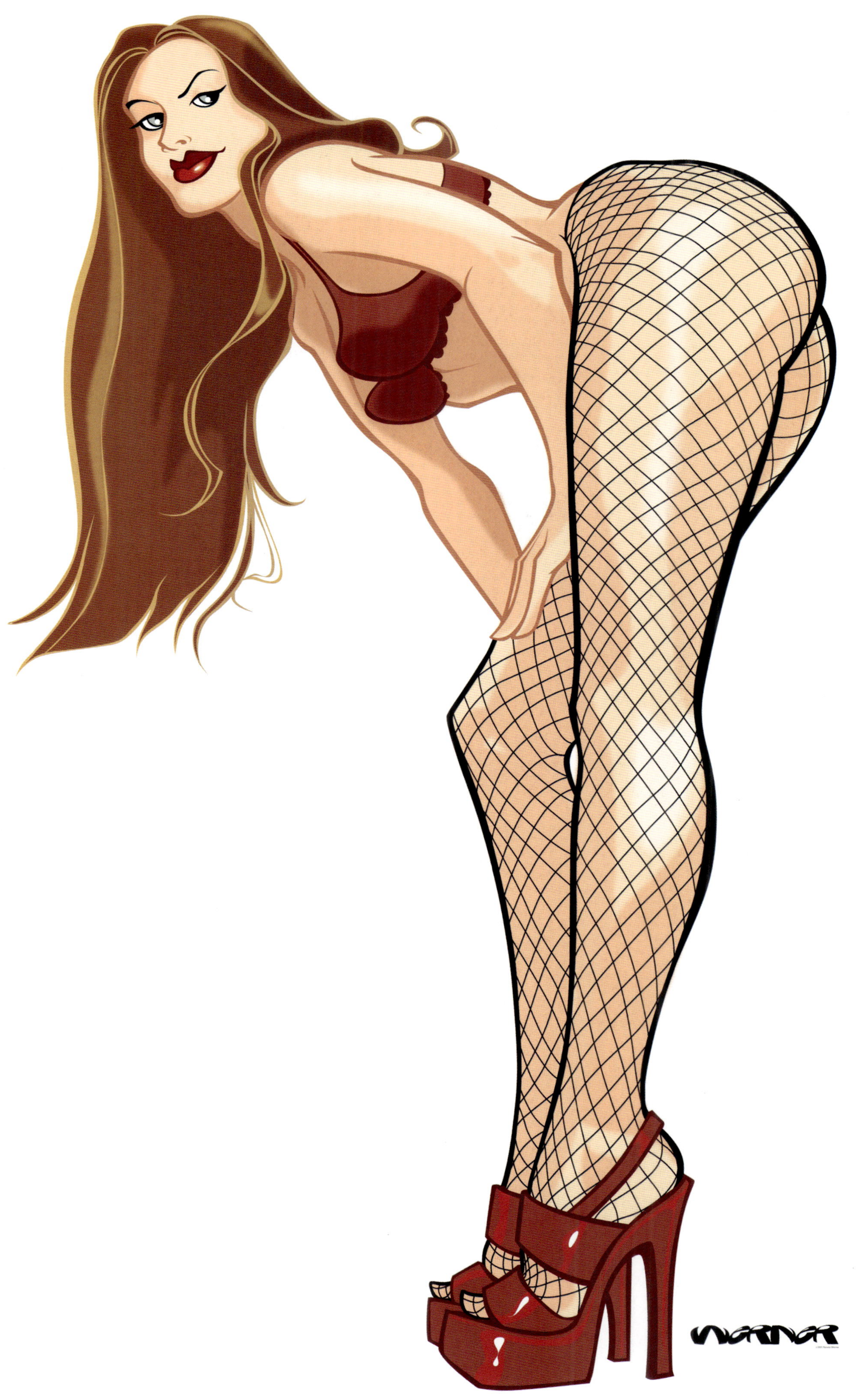
WERNER

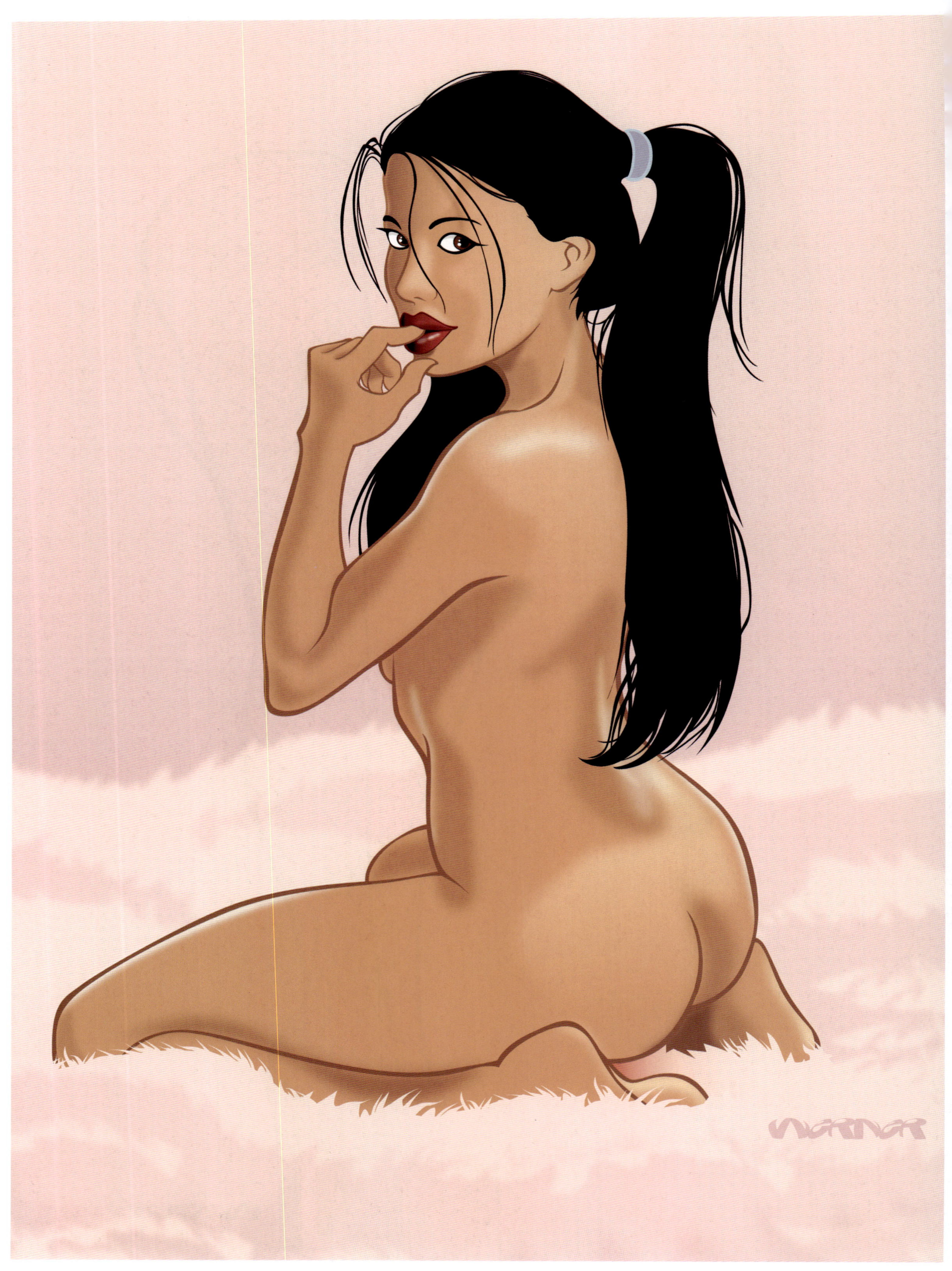

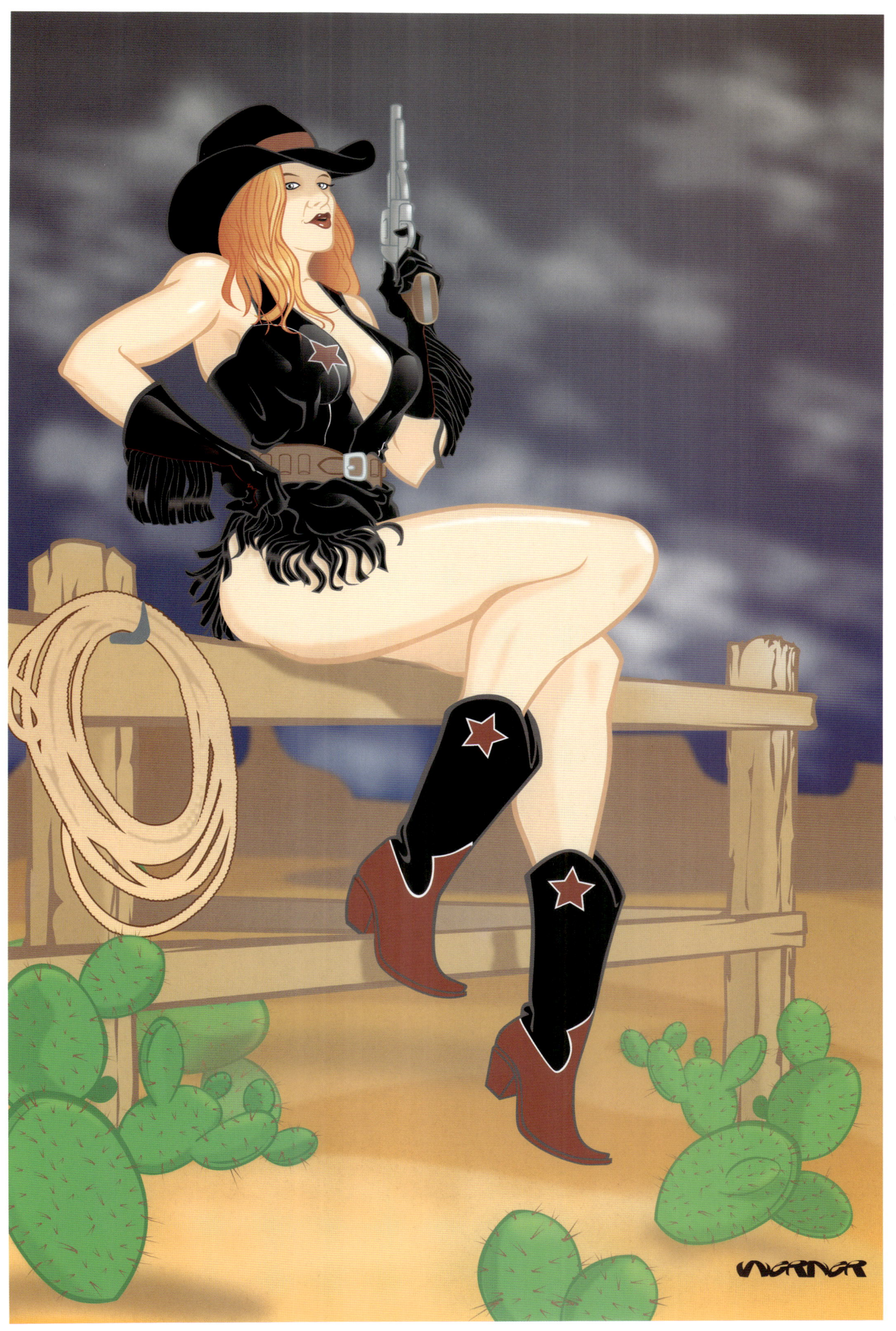
WERNER

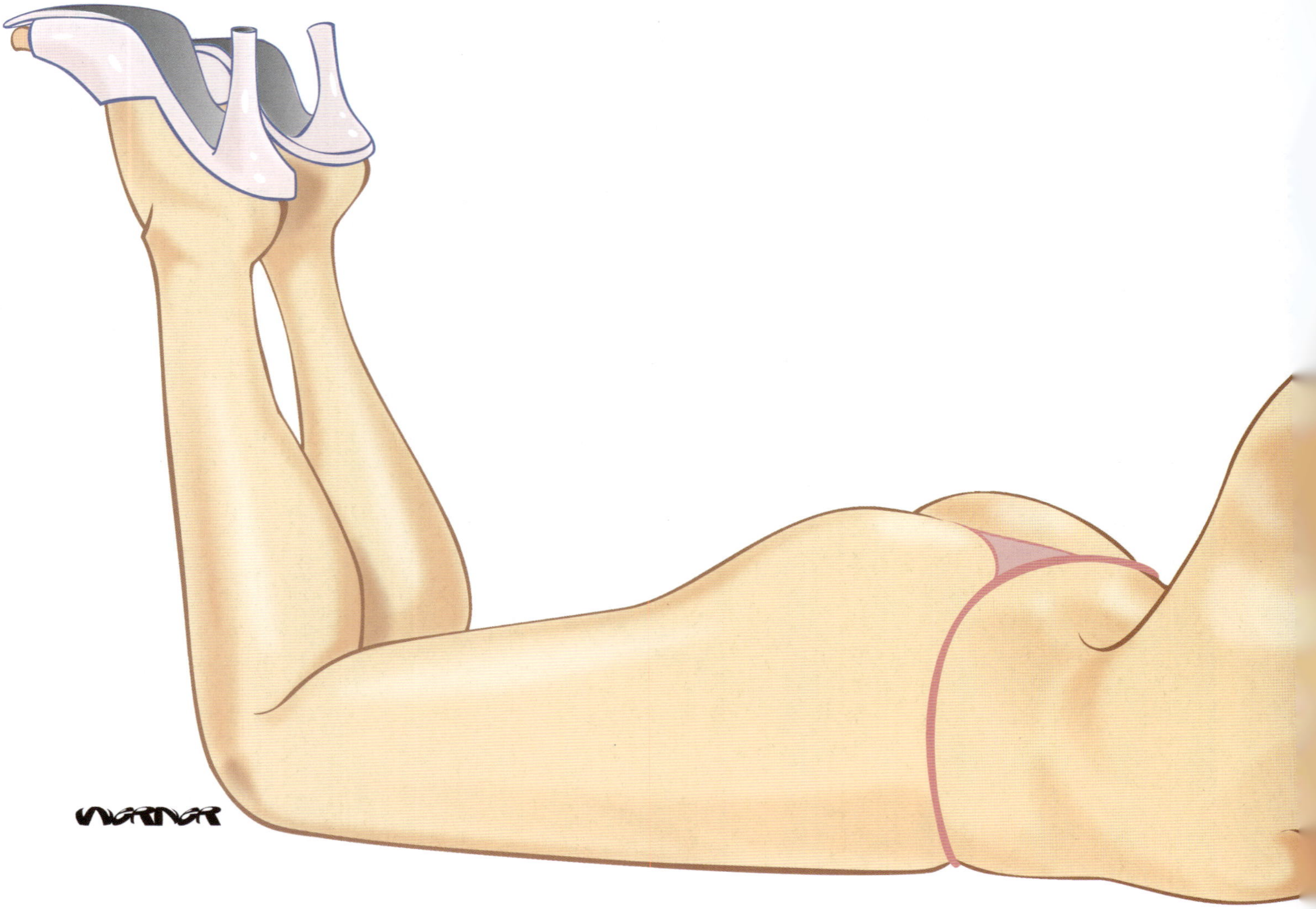

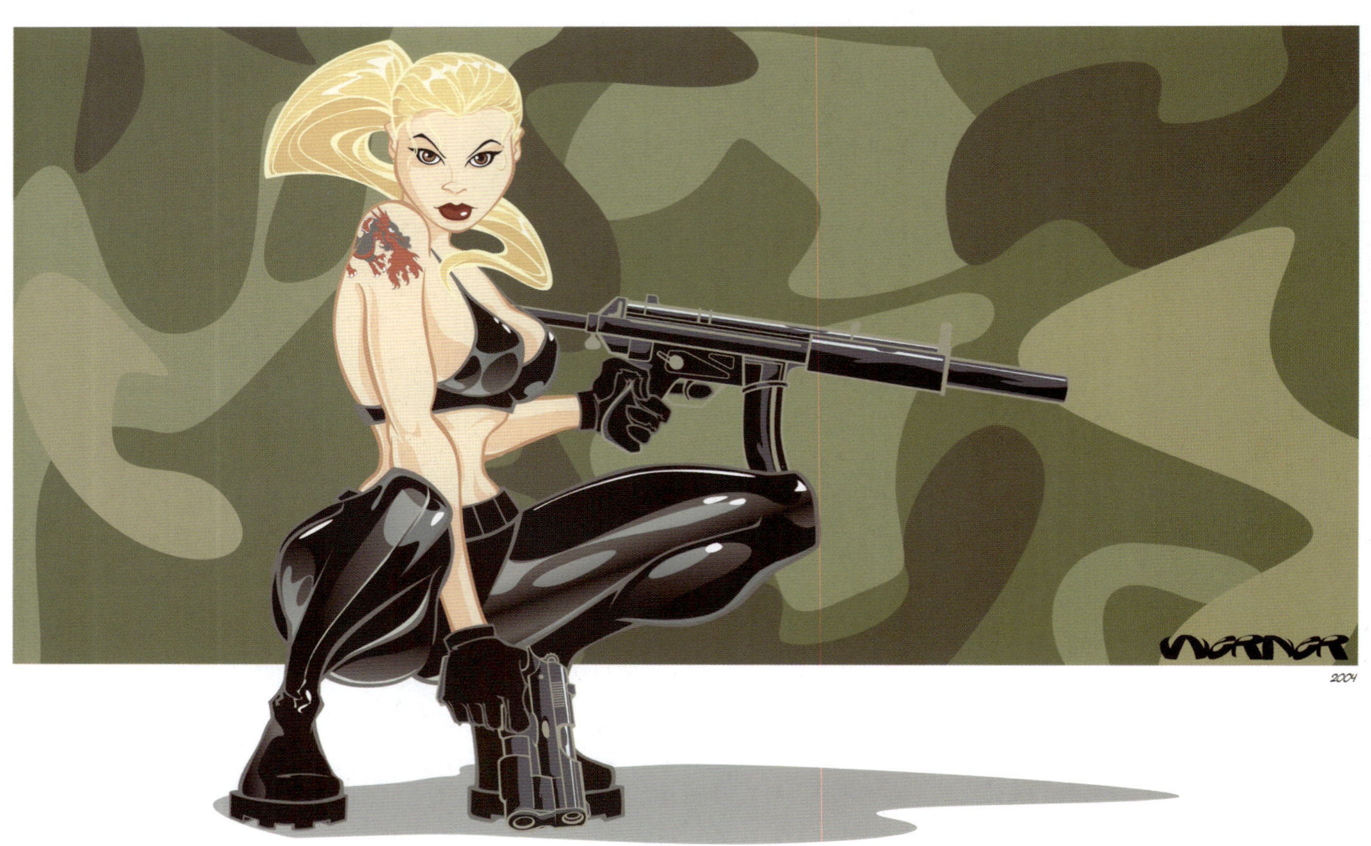
2004

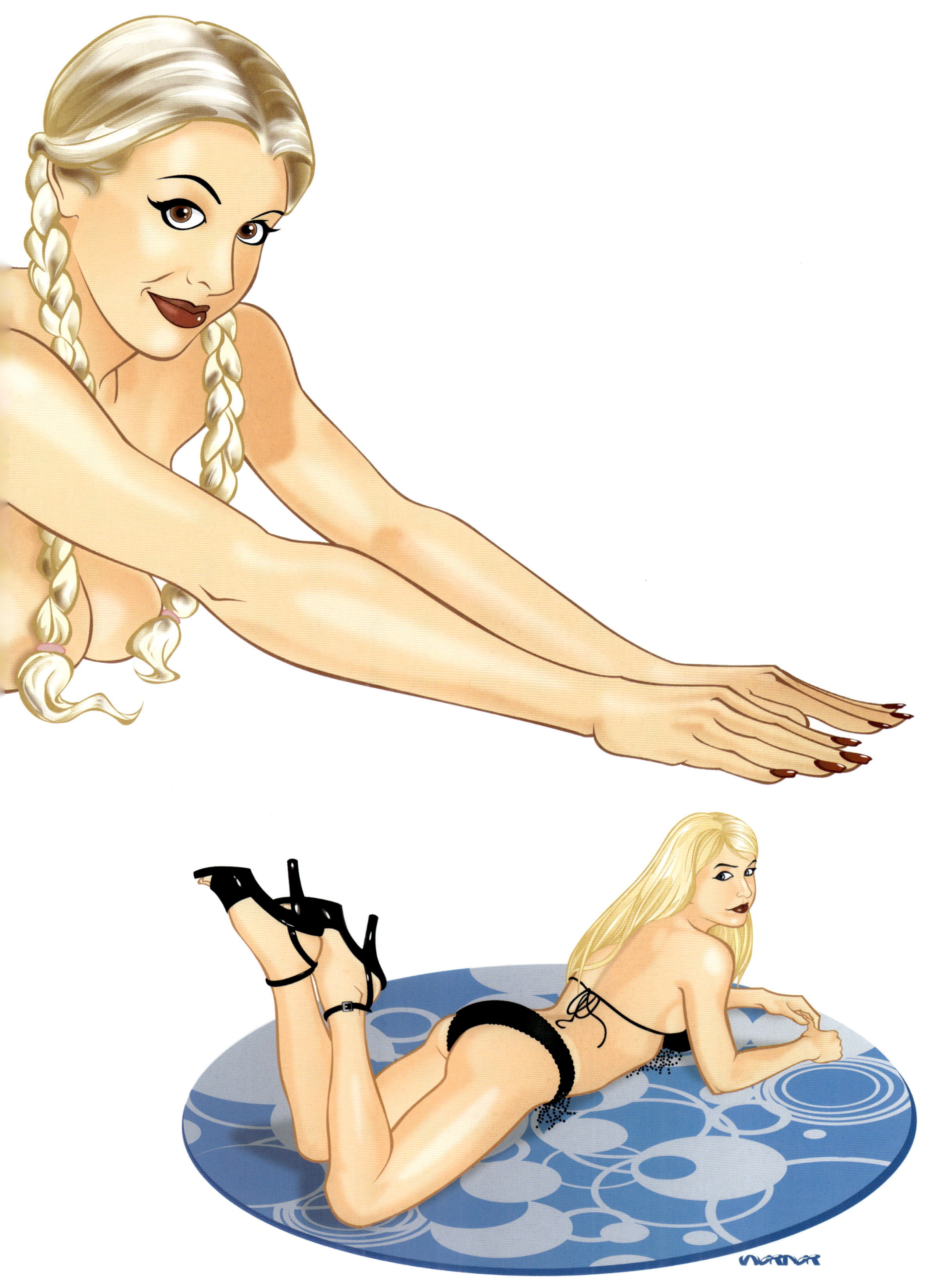
Werner

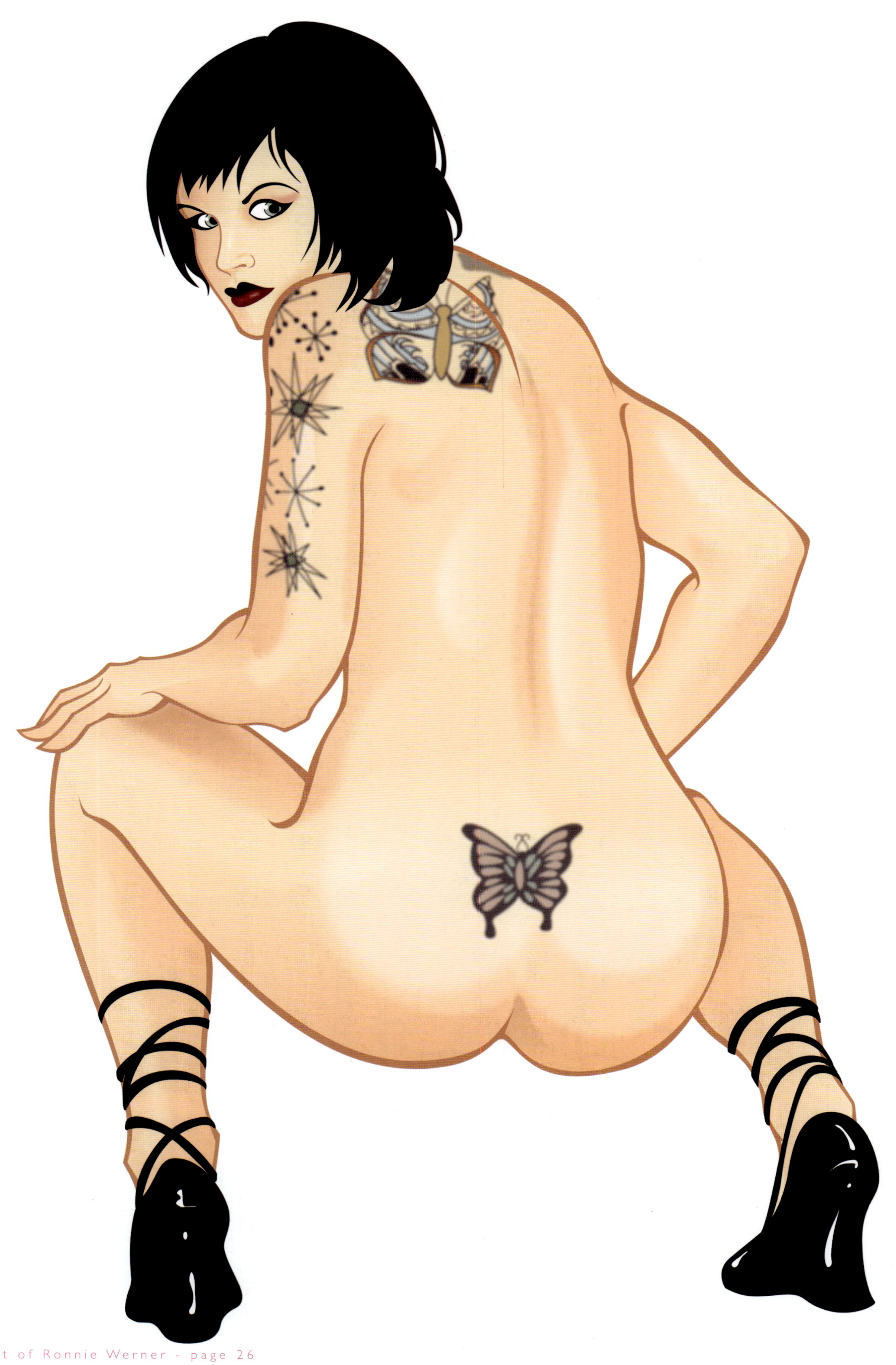

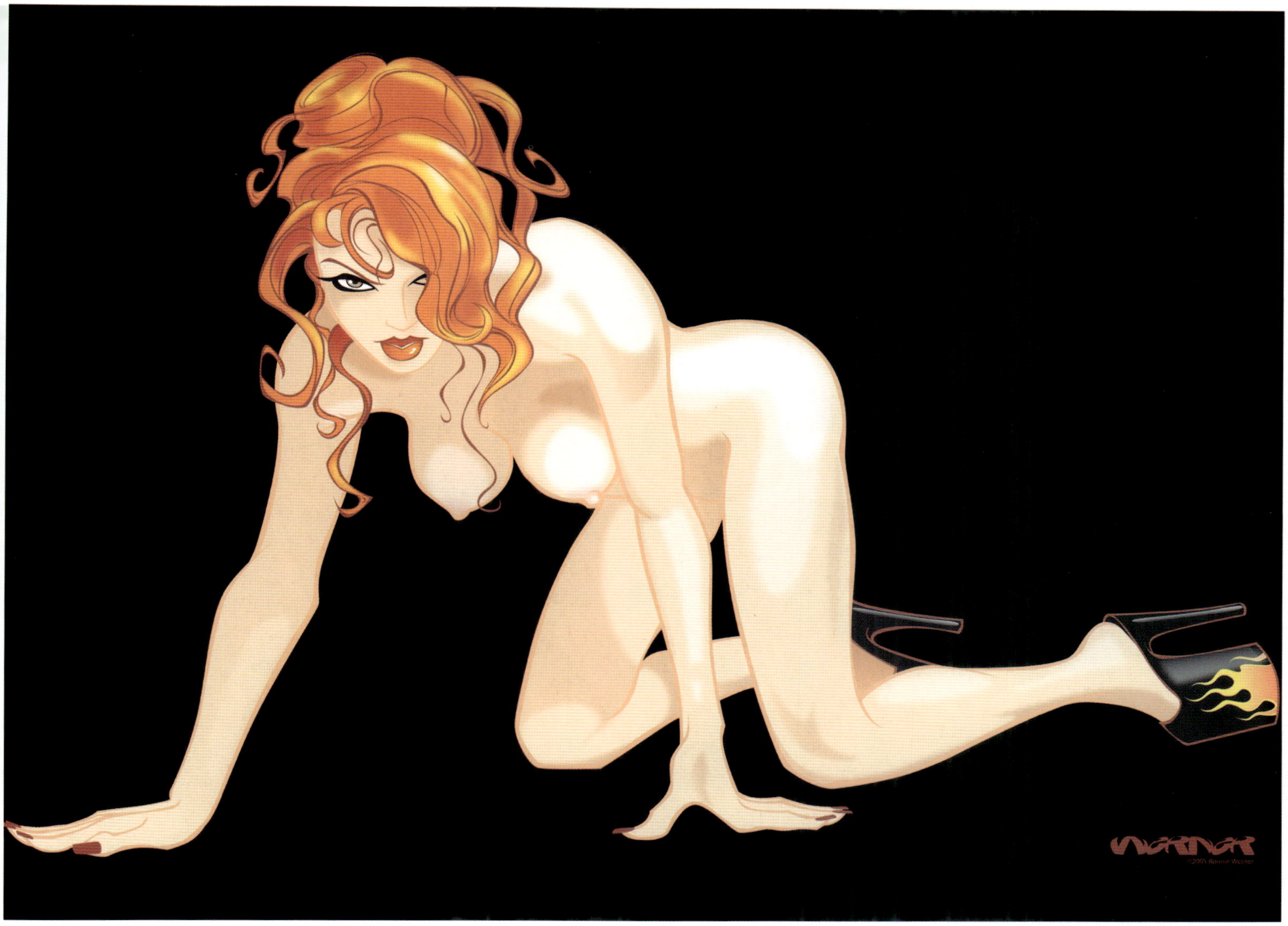

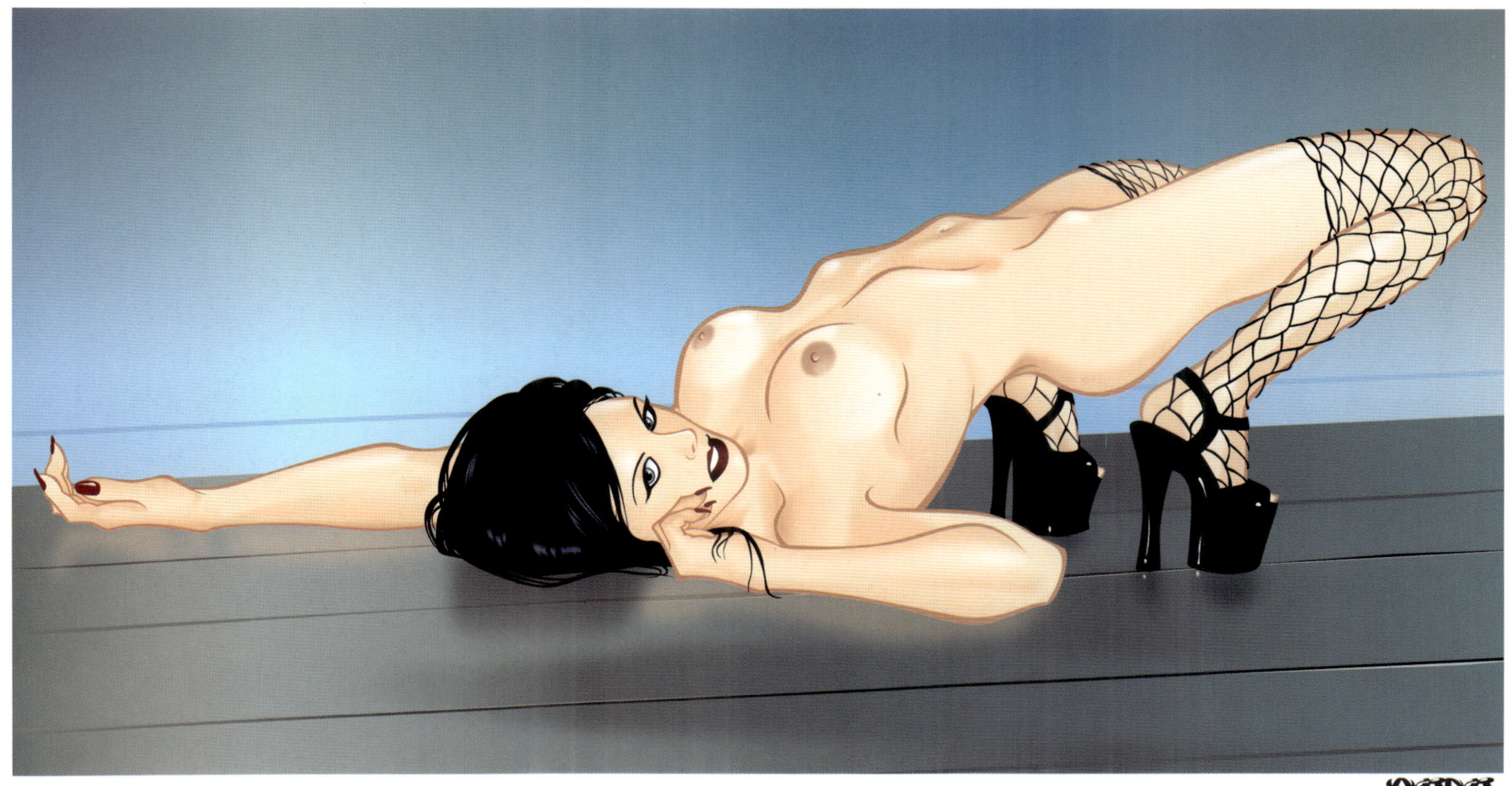

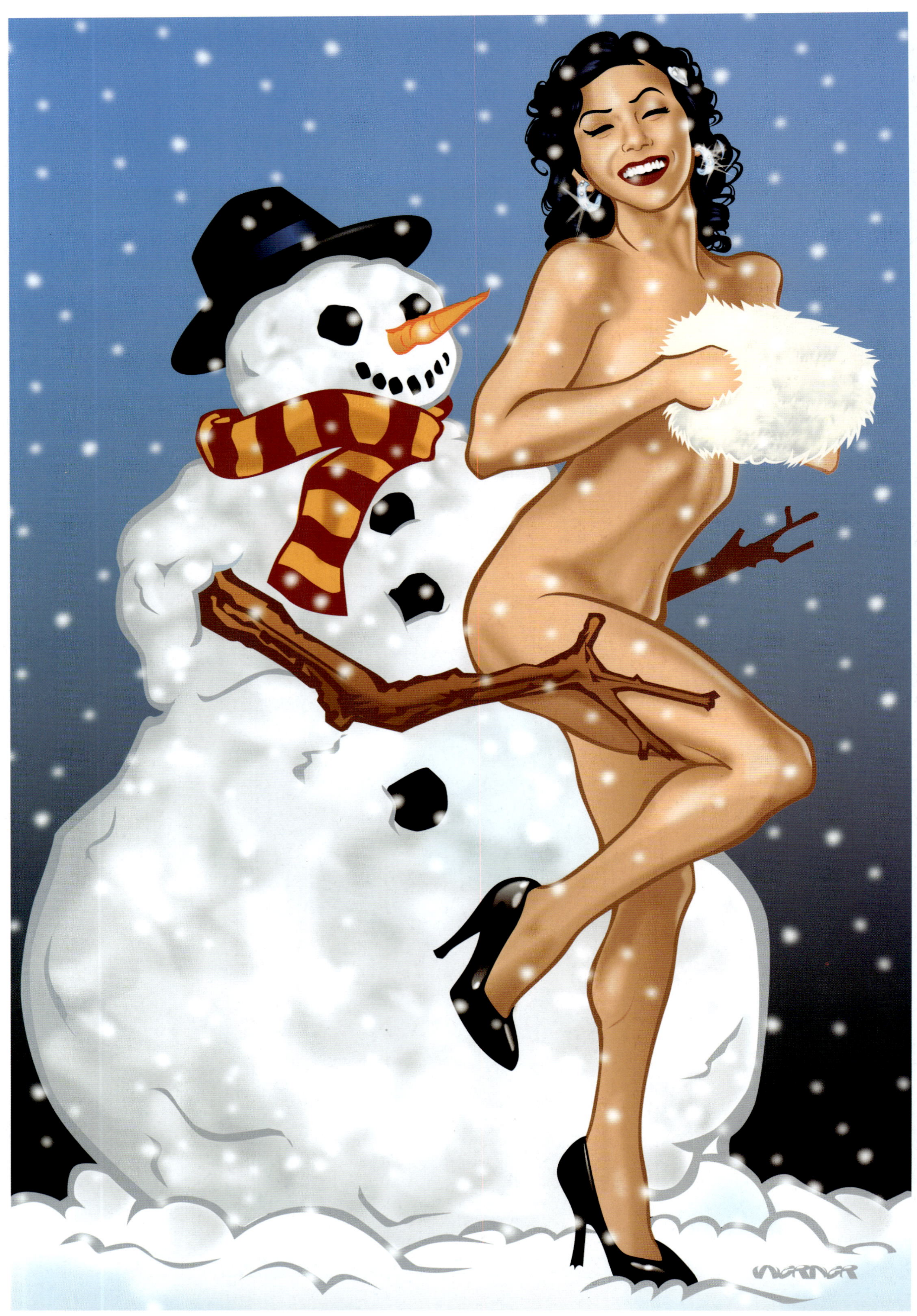
WERNER

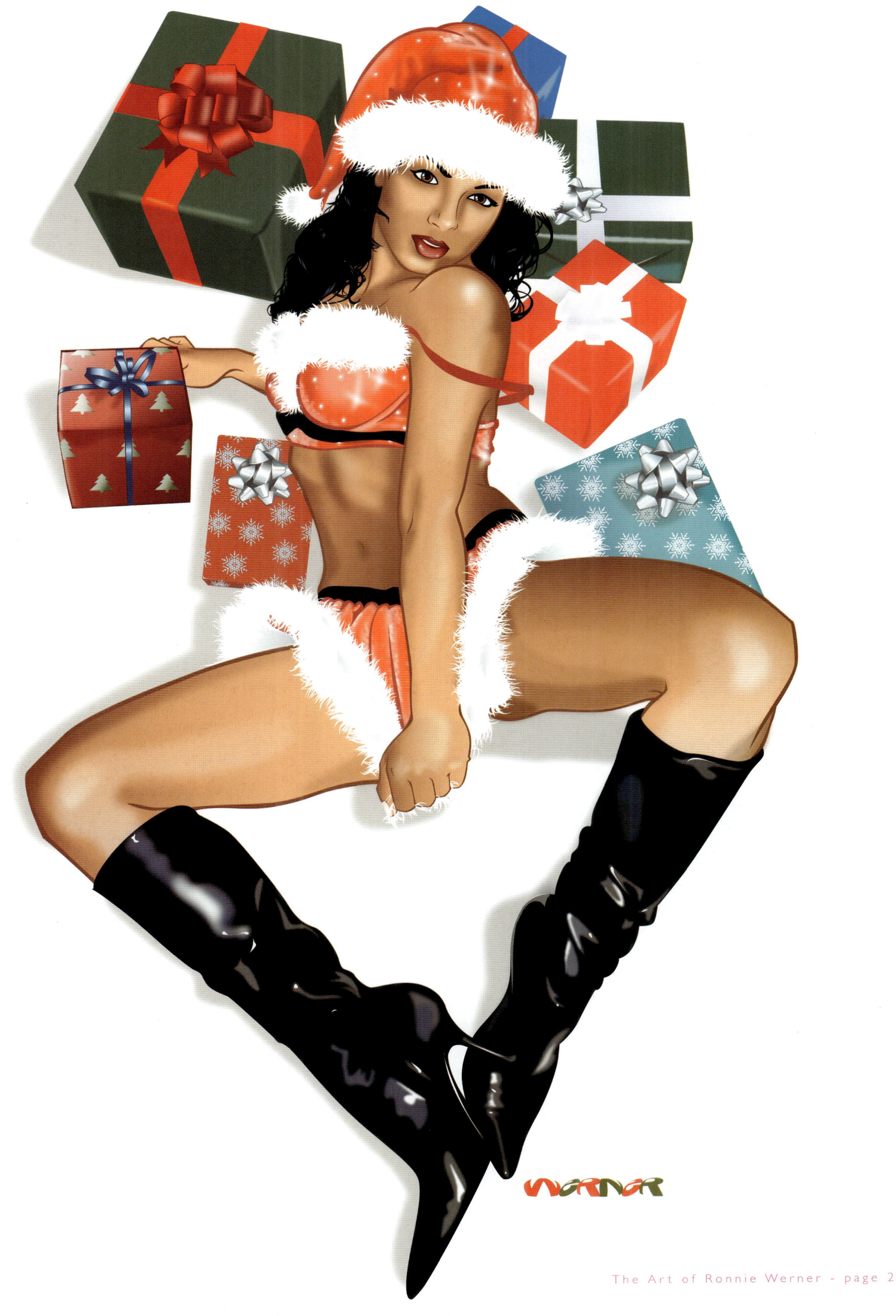
WERNER

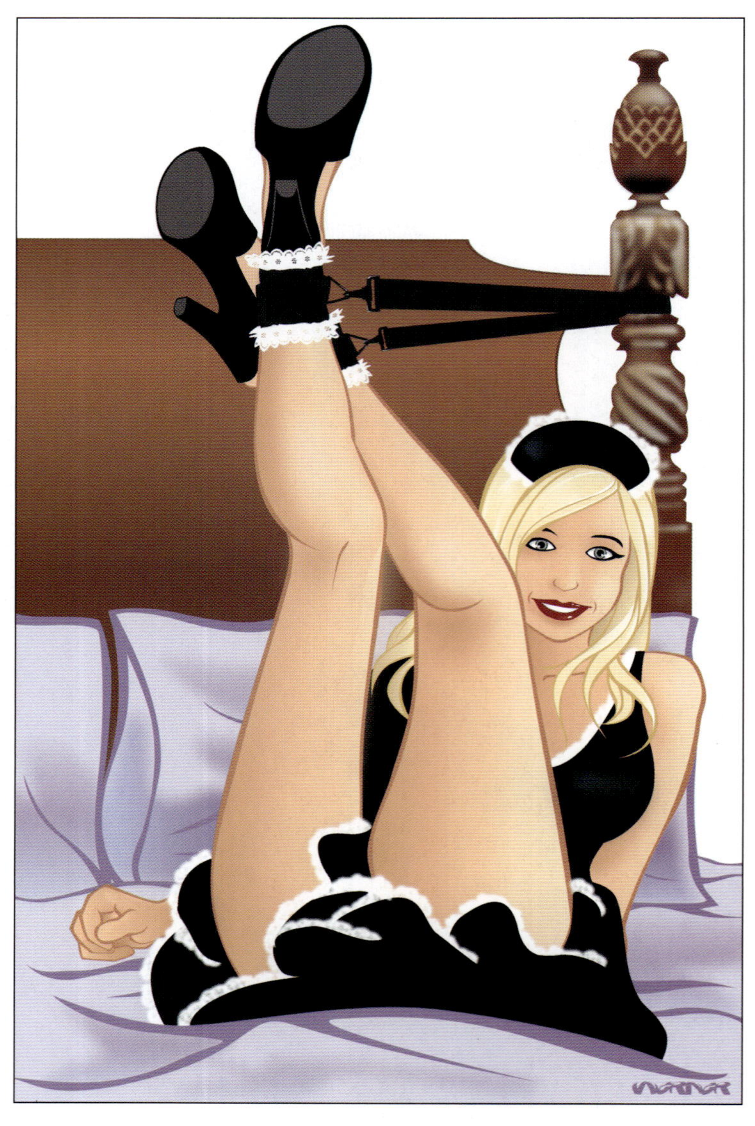

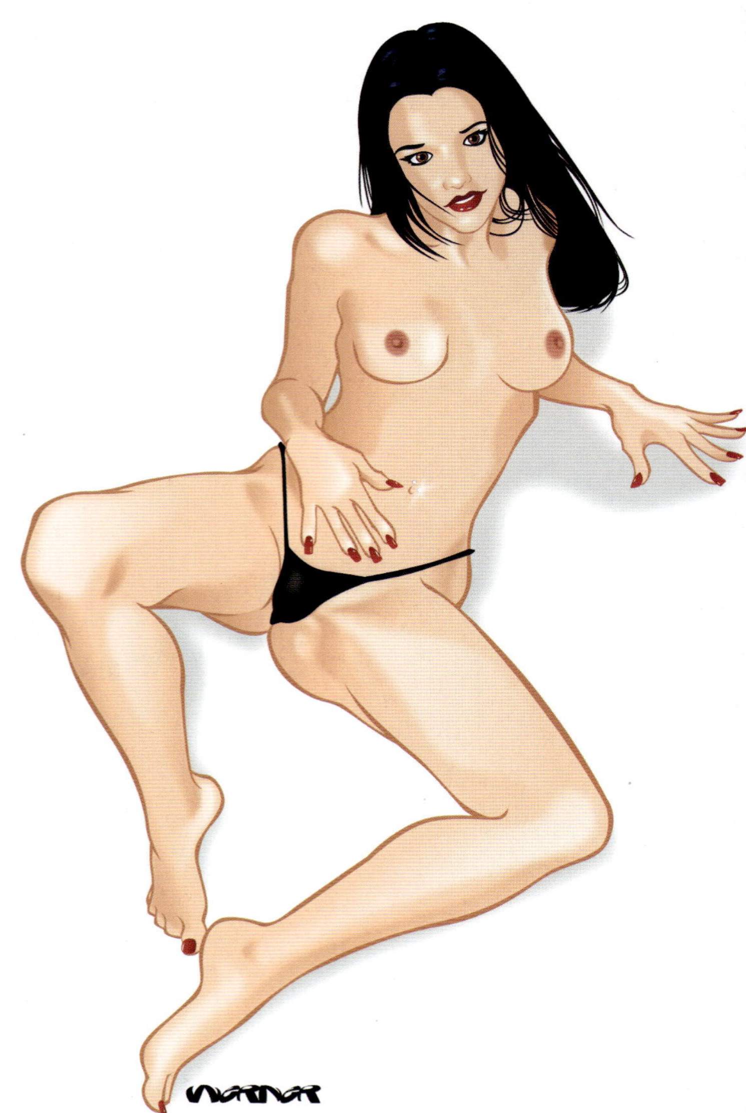

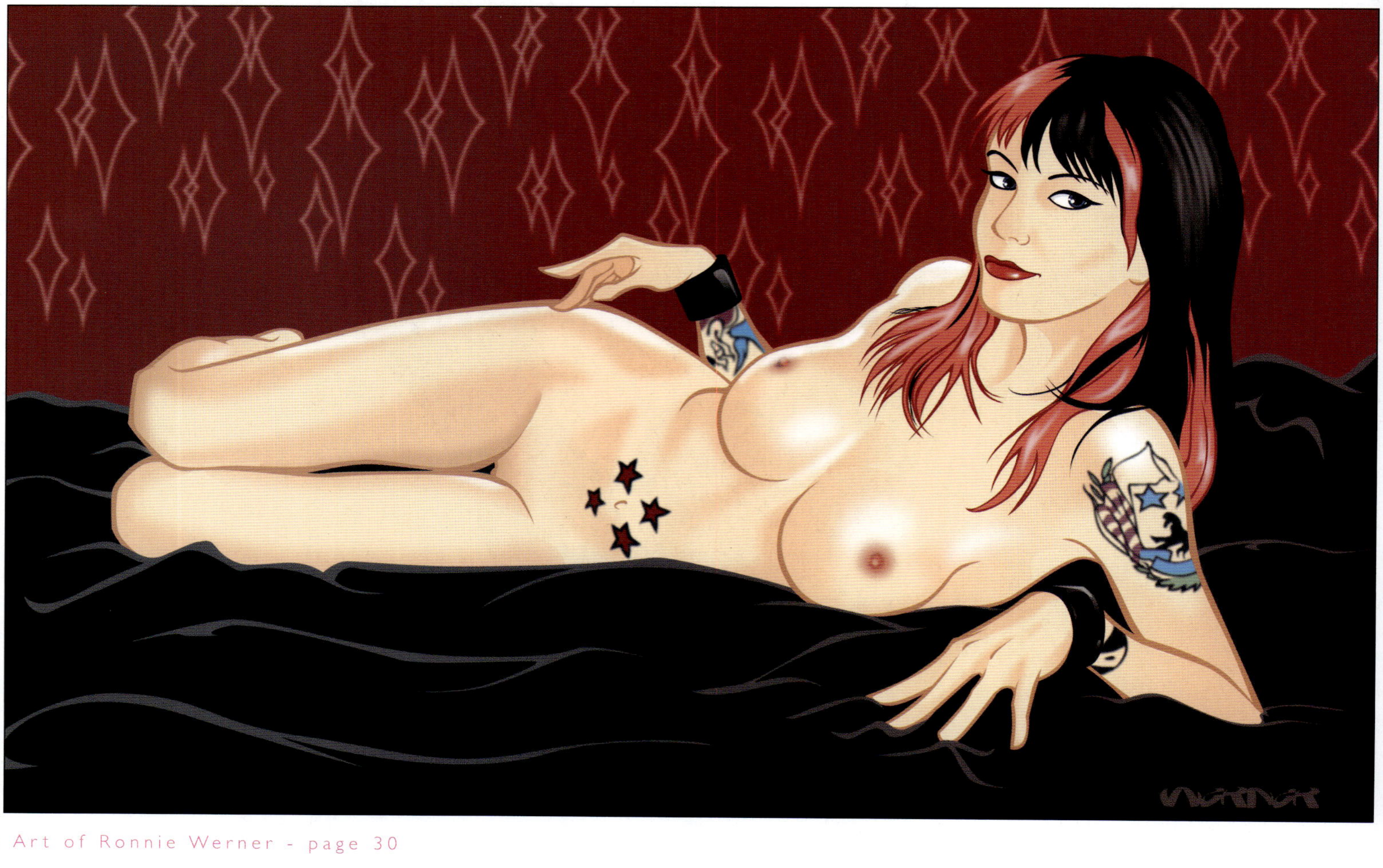

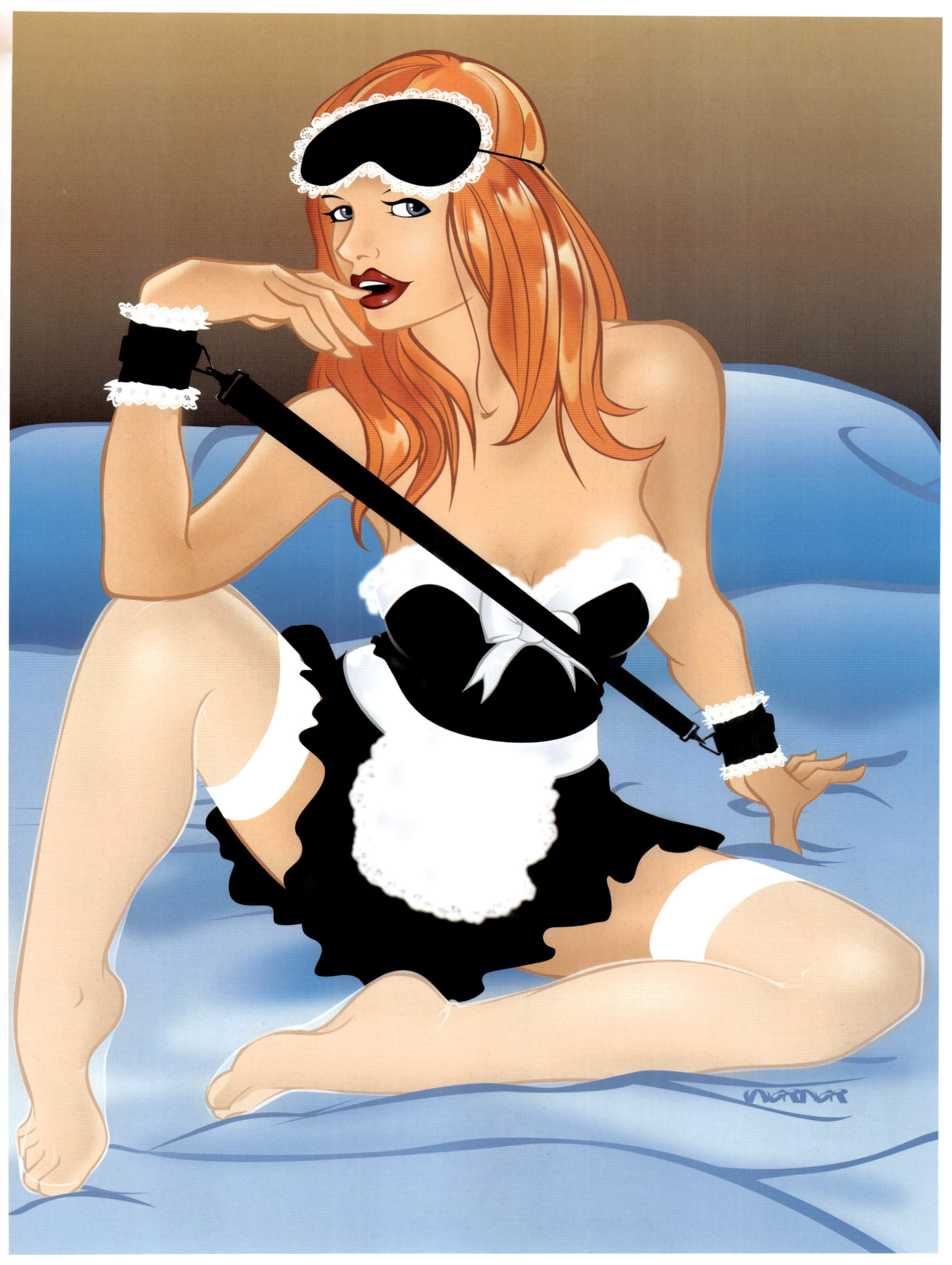

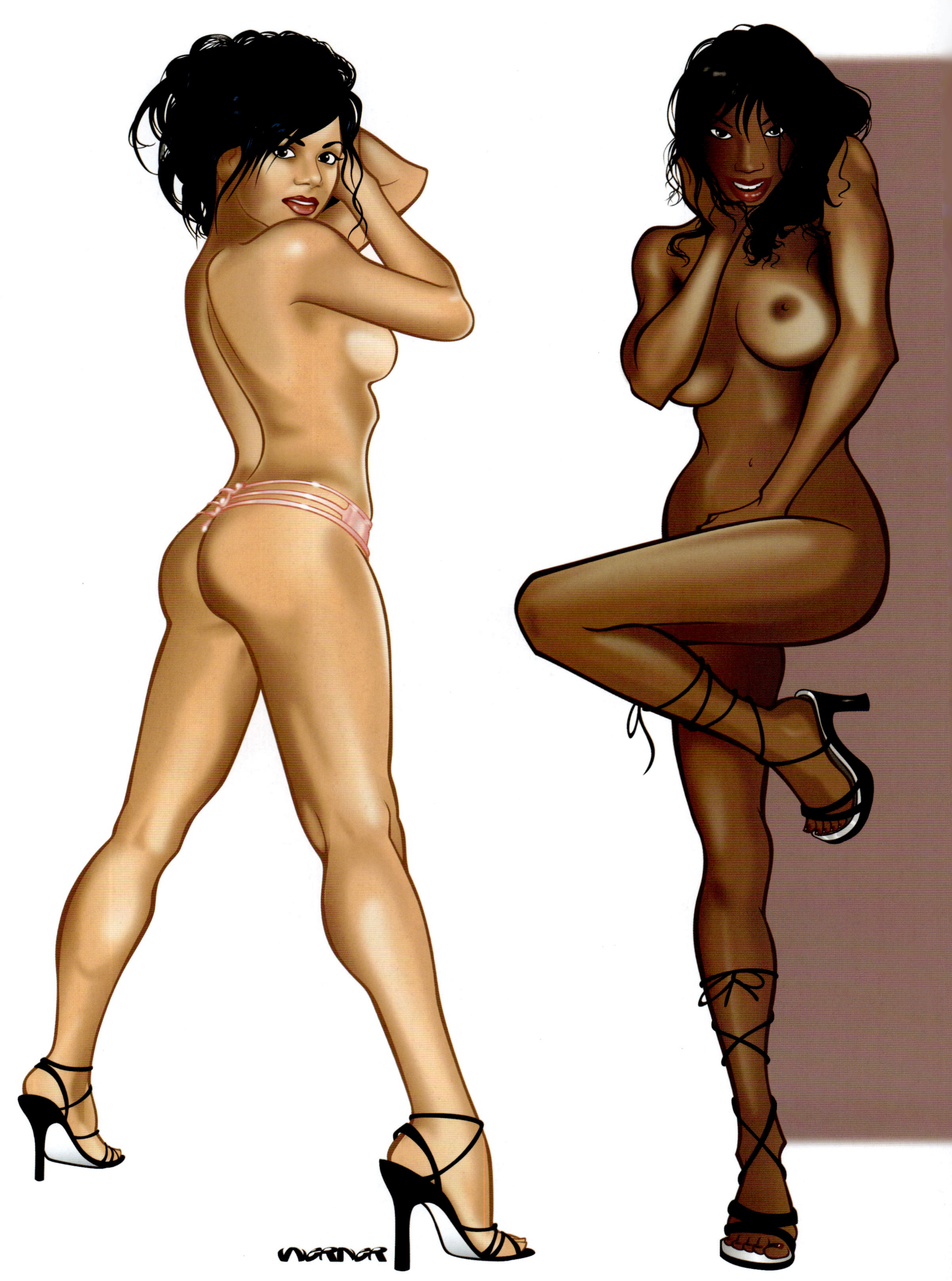

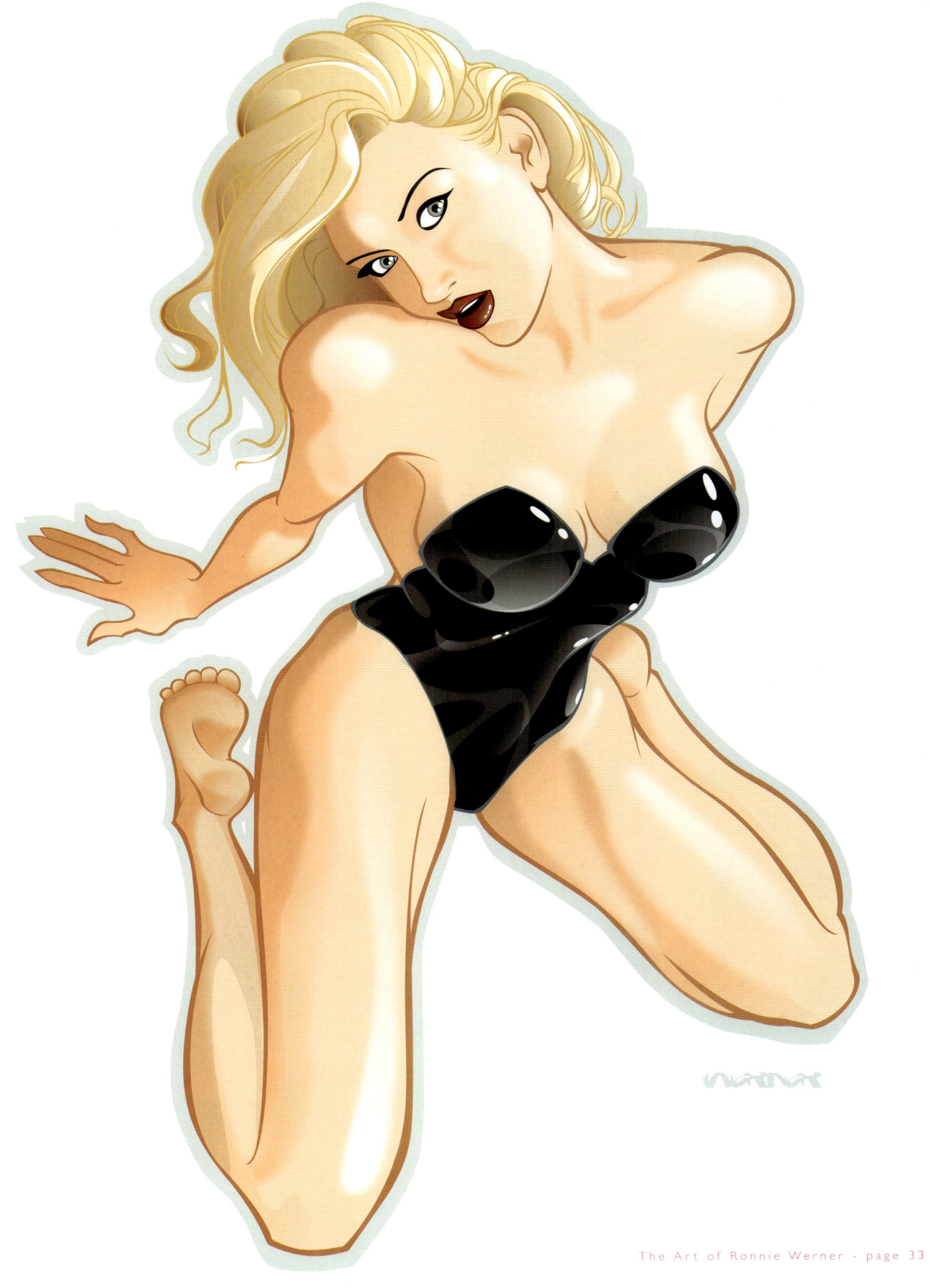

werner

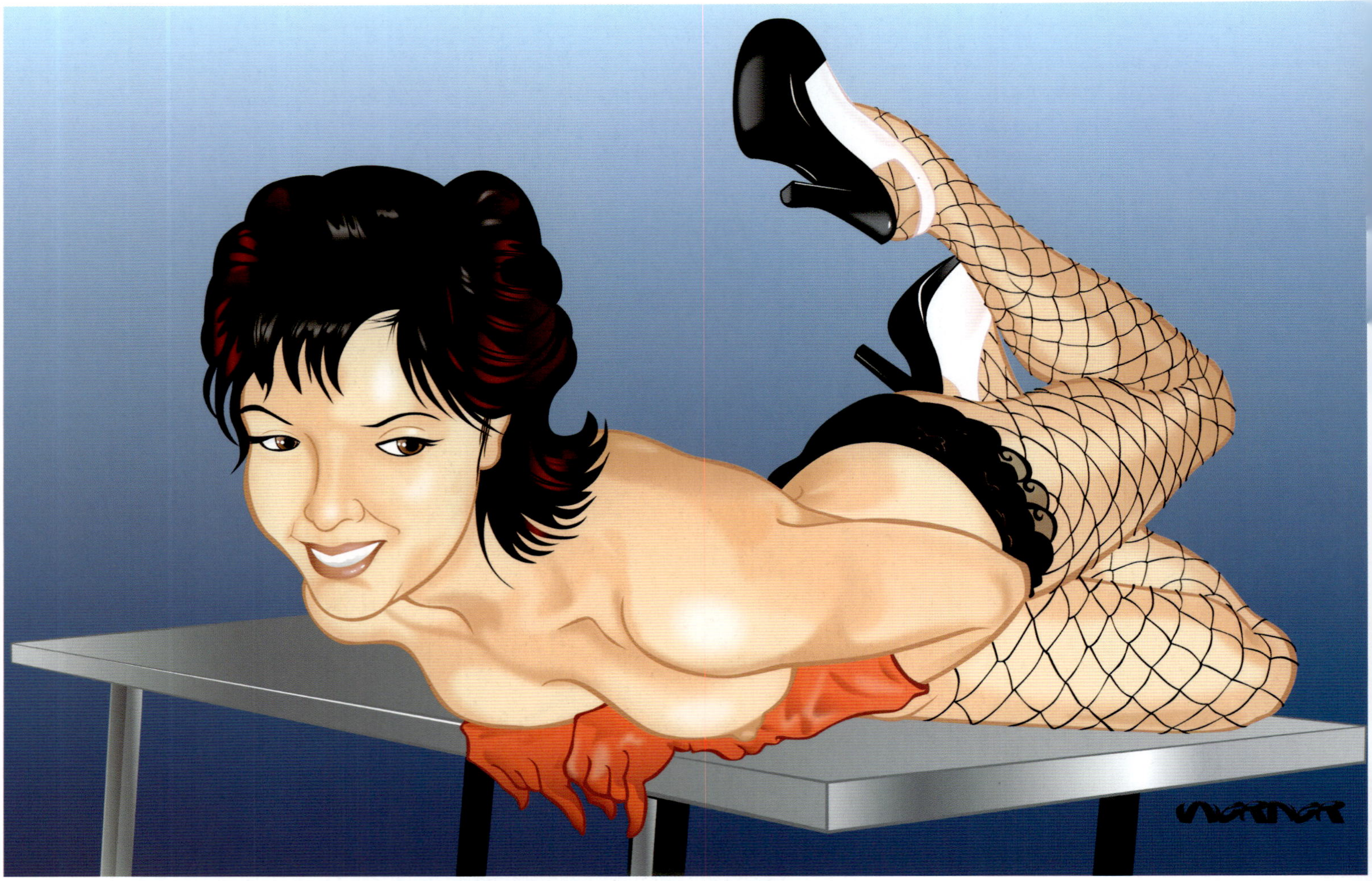

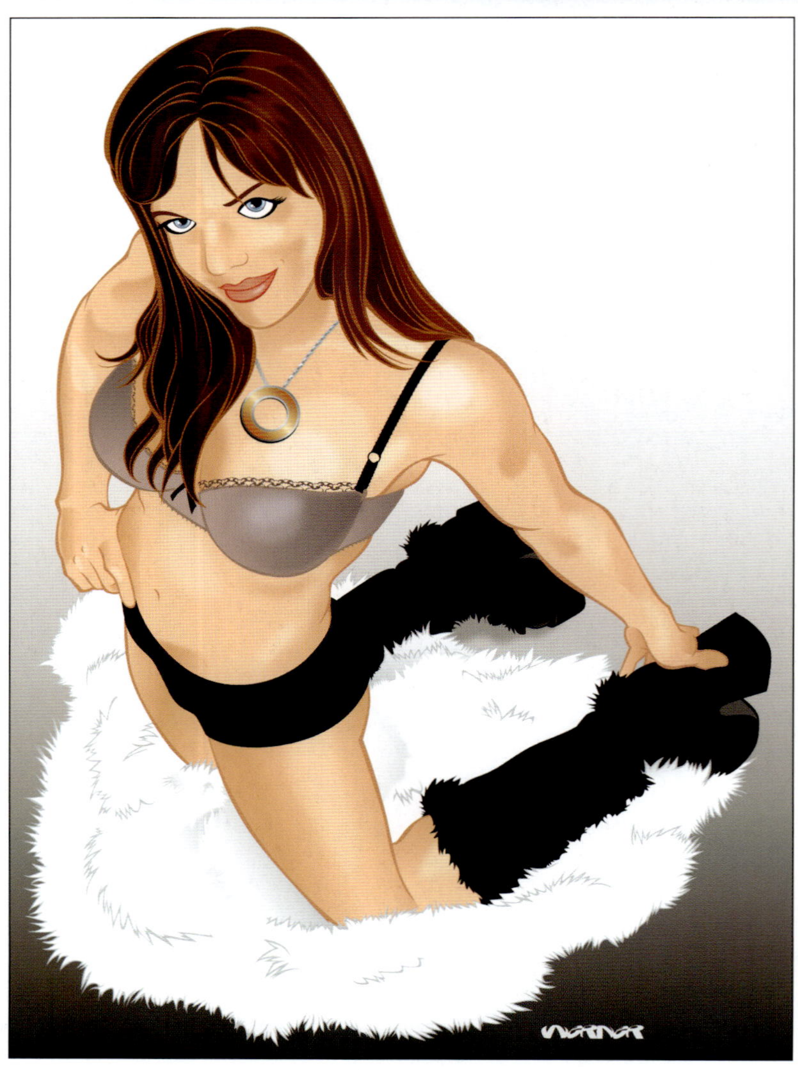

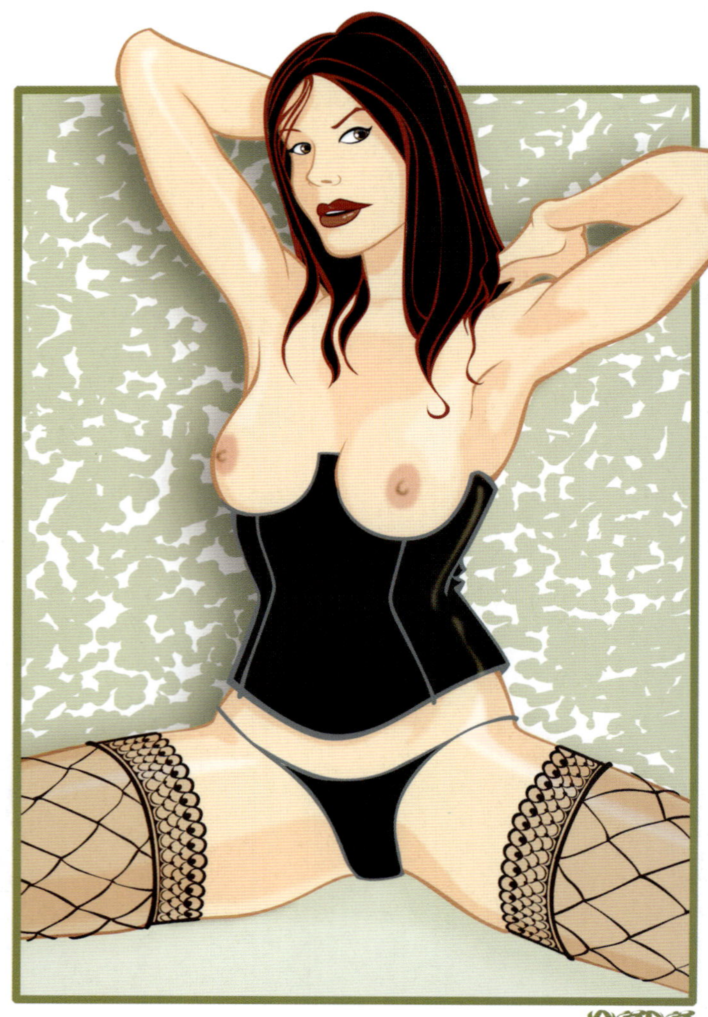

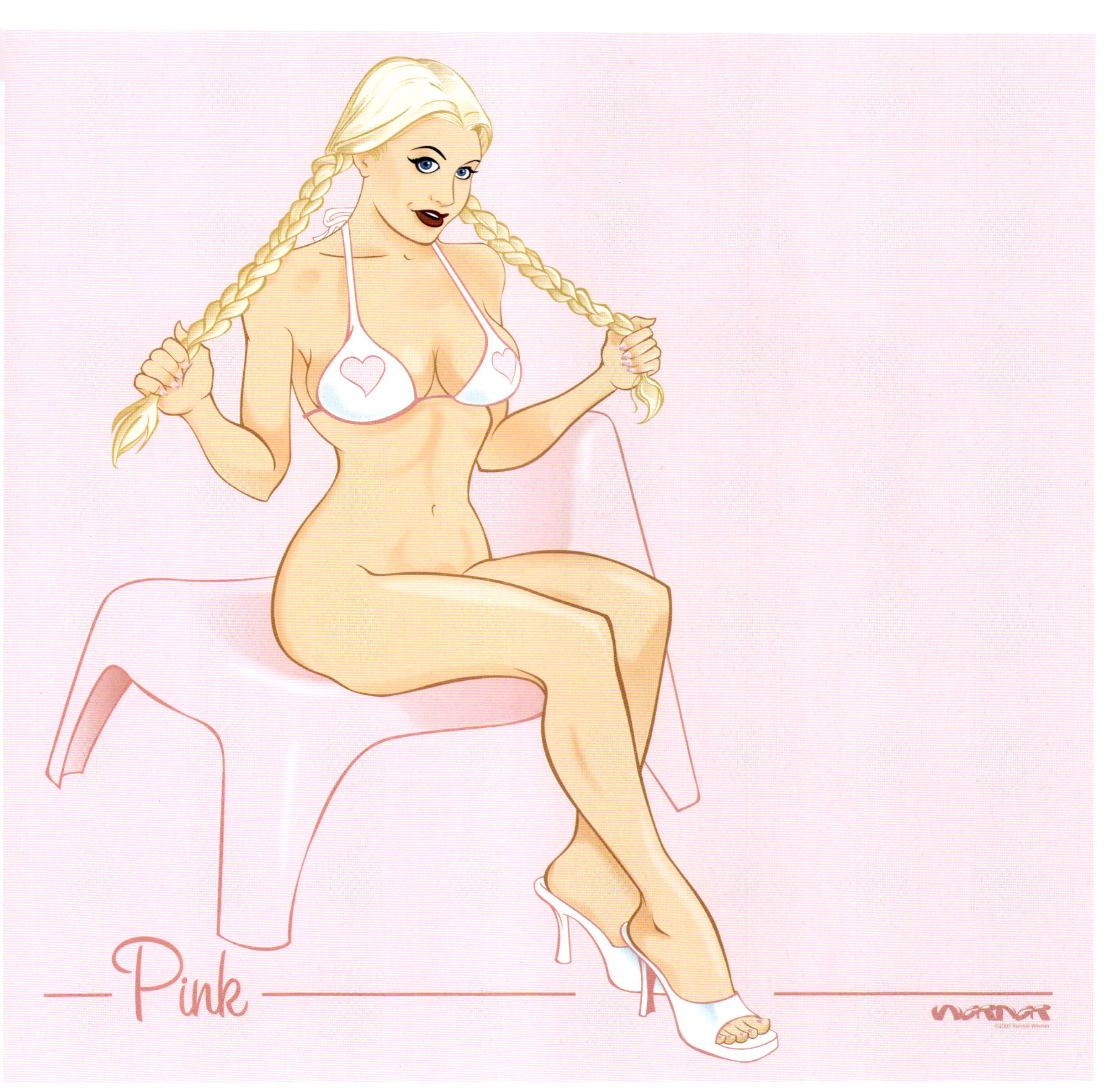
Pink
Werner
©2005 Ronnie Werner

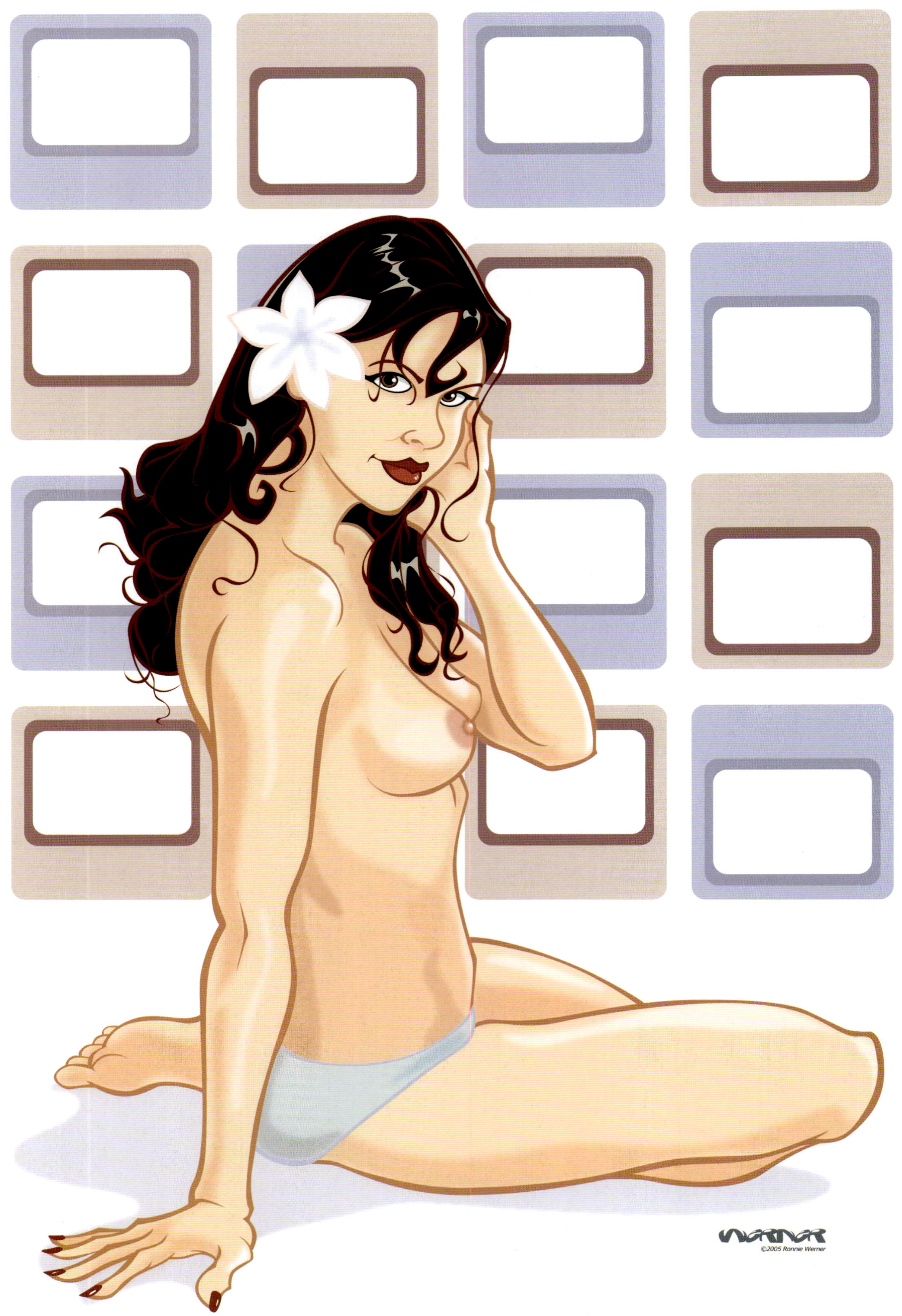
WERNER
©2005 Ronnie Werner

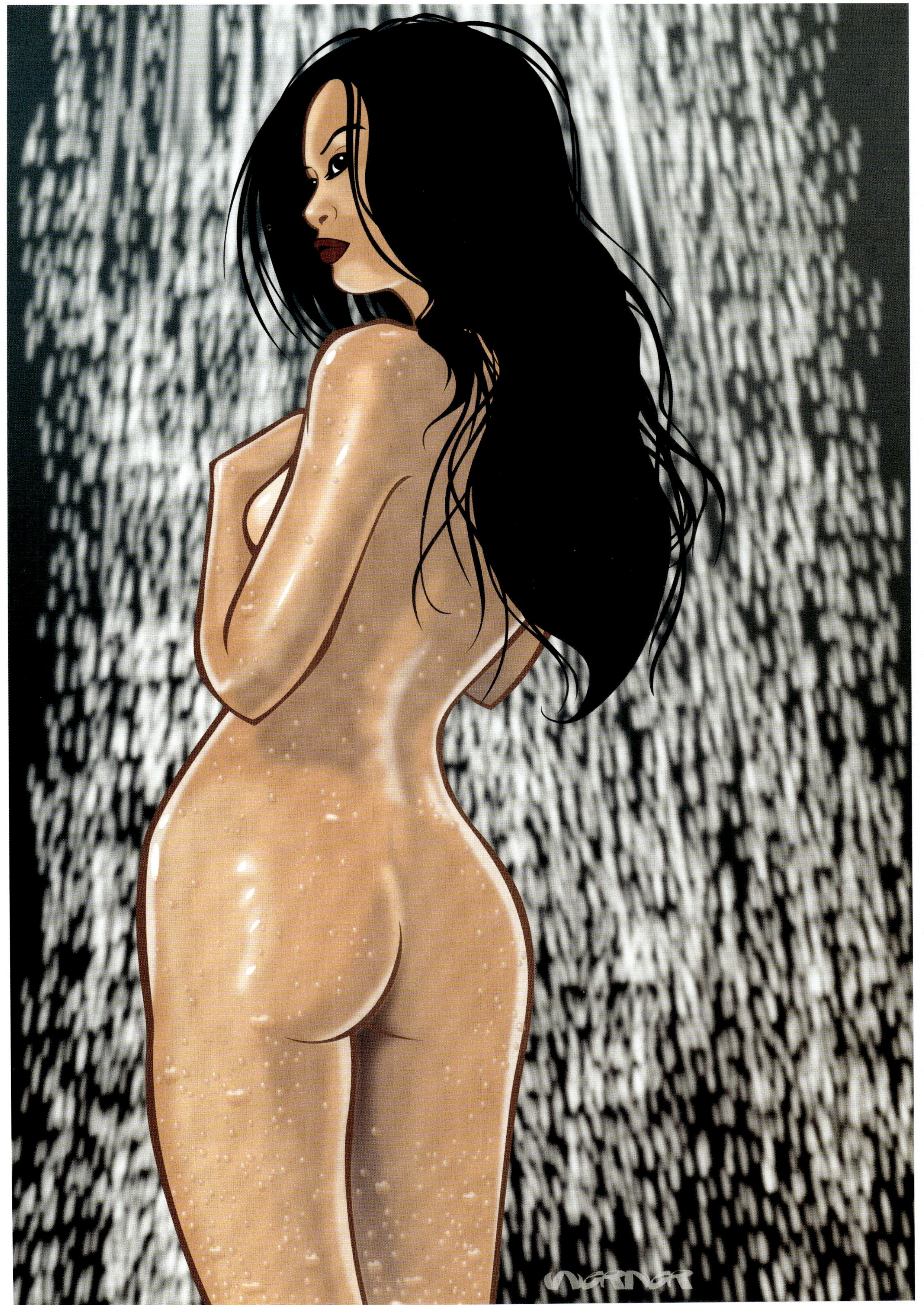

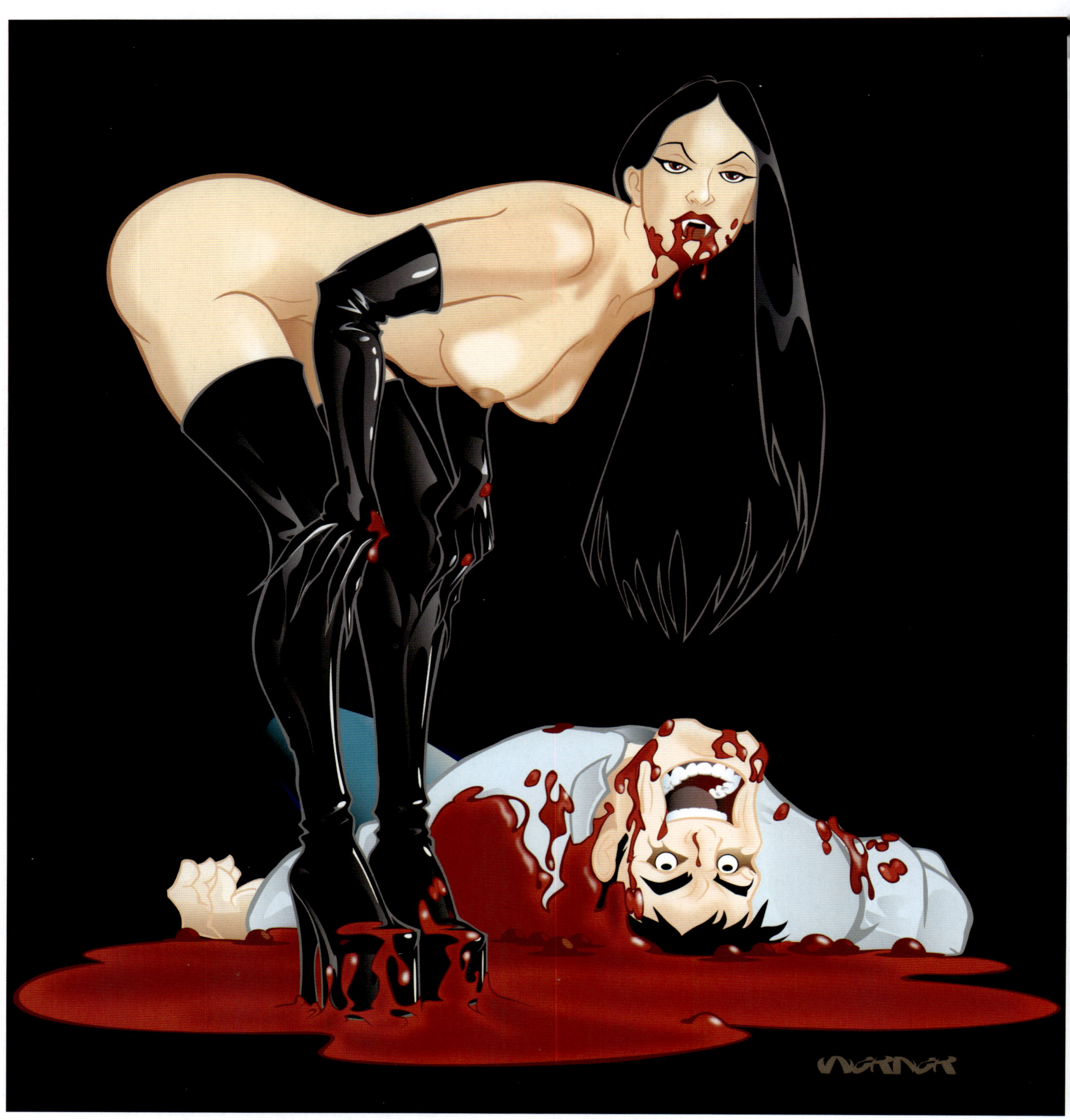

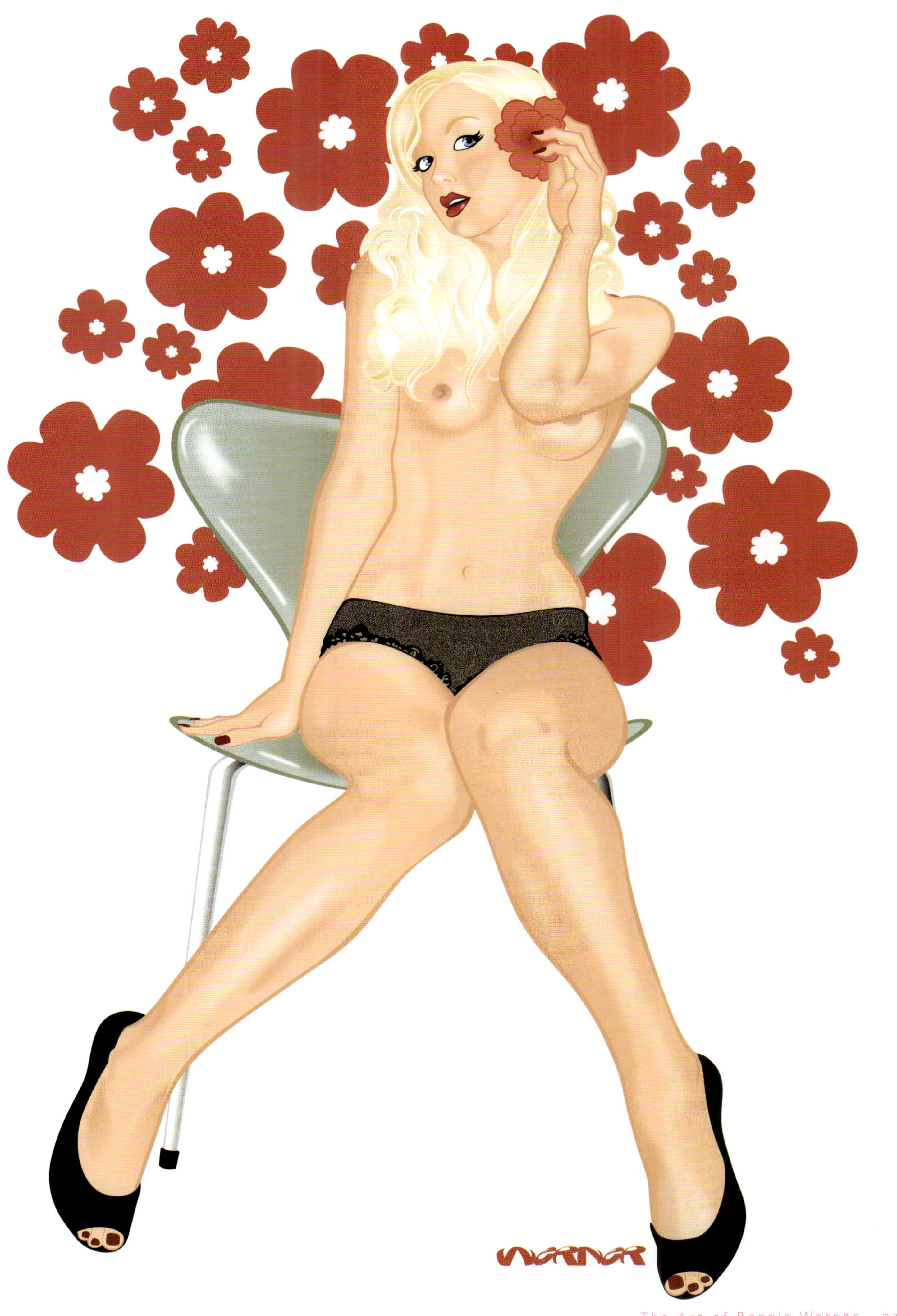
WERNER

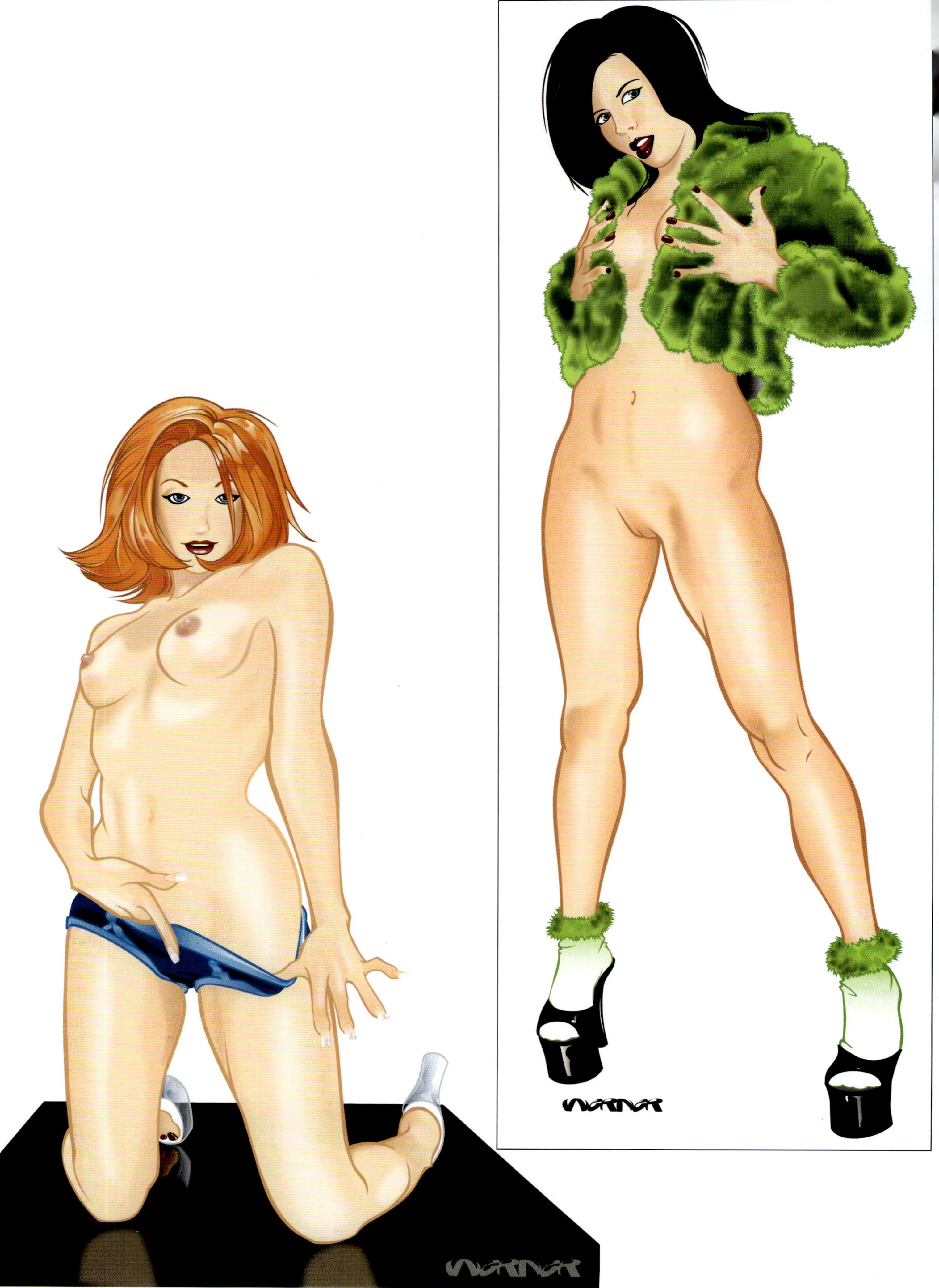
WERNER
WERNER

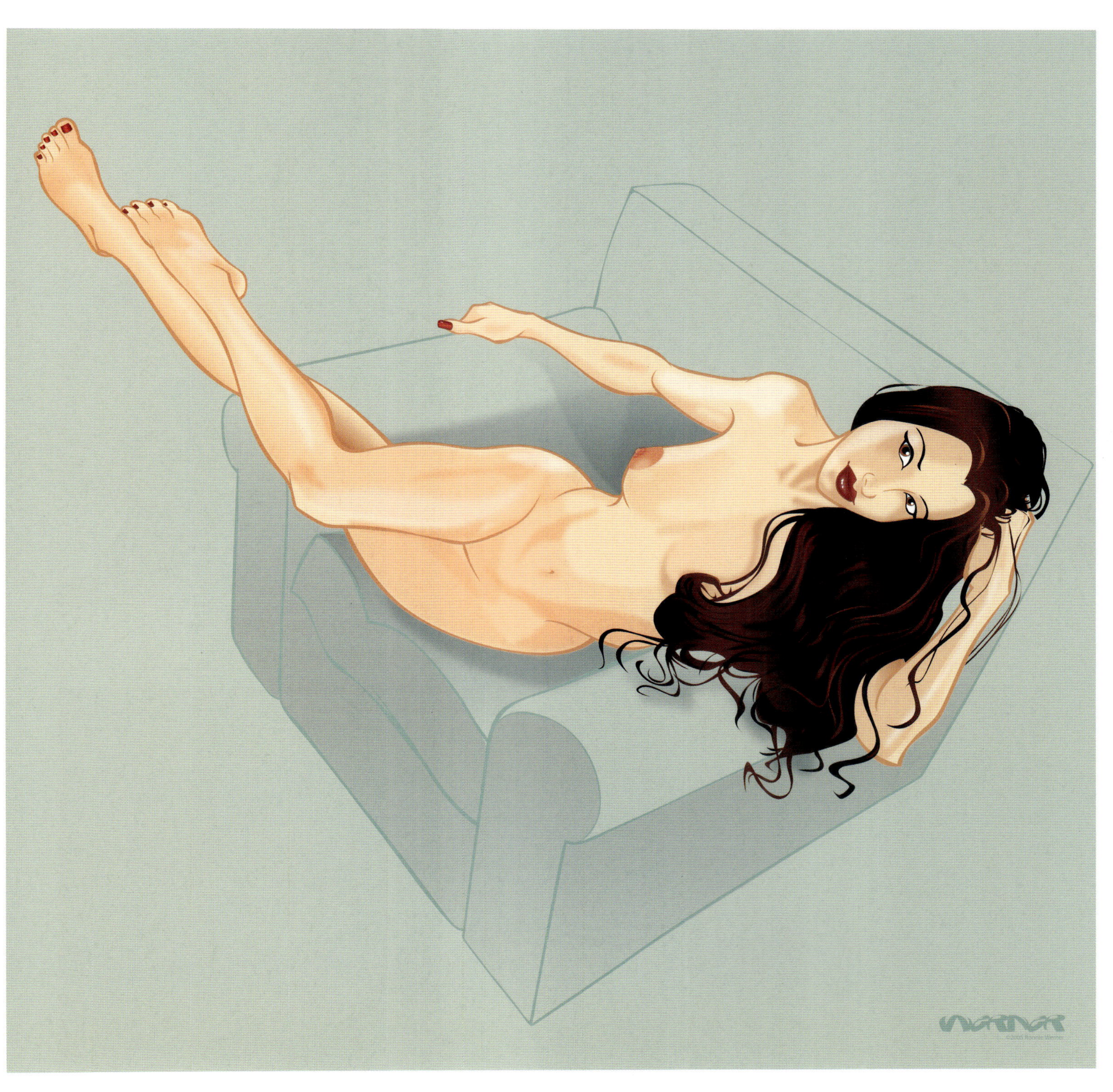

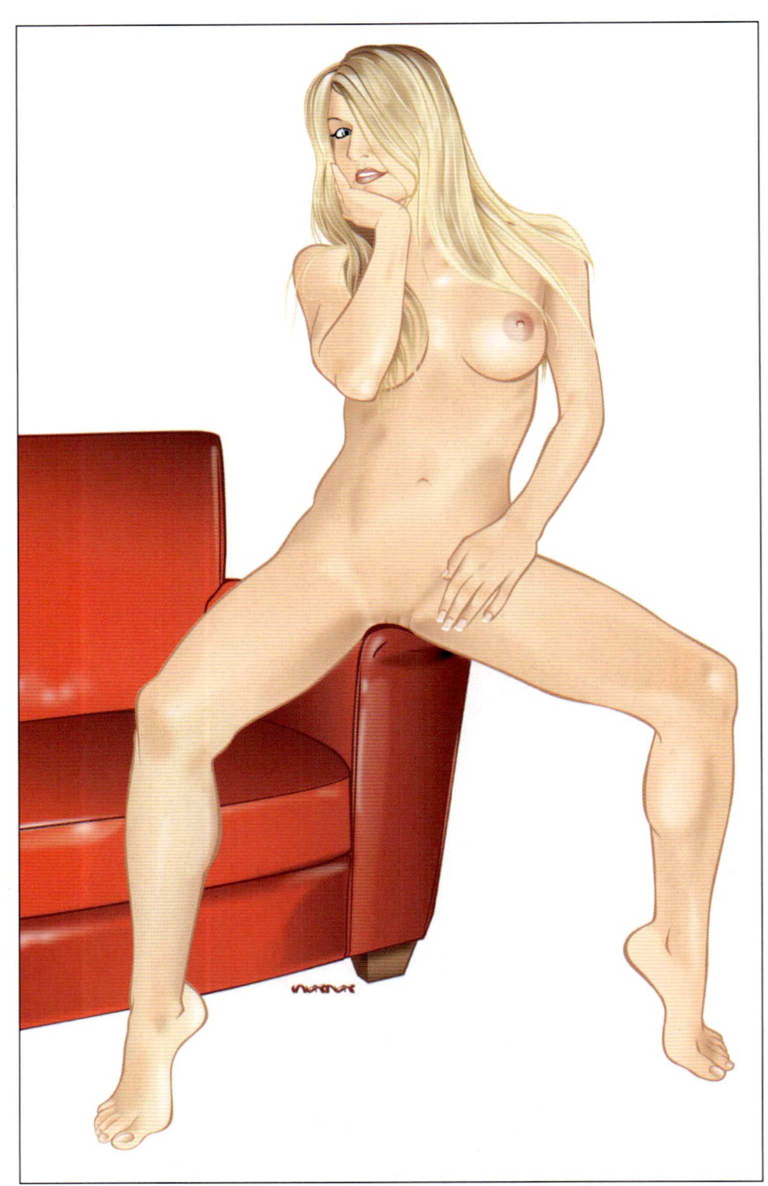

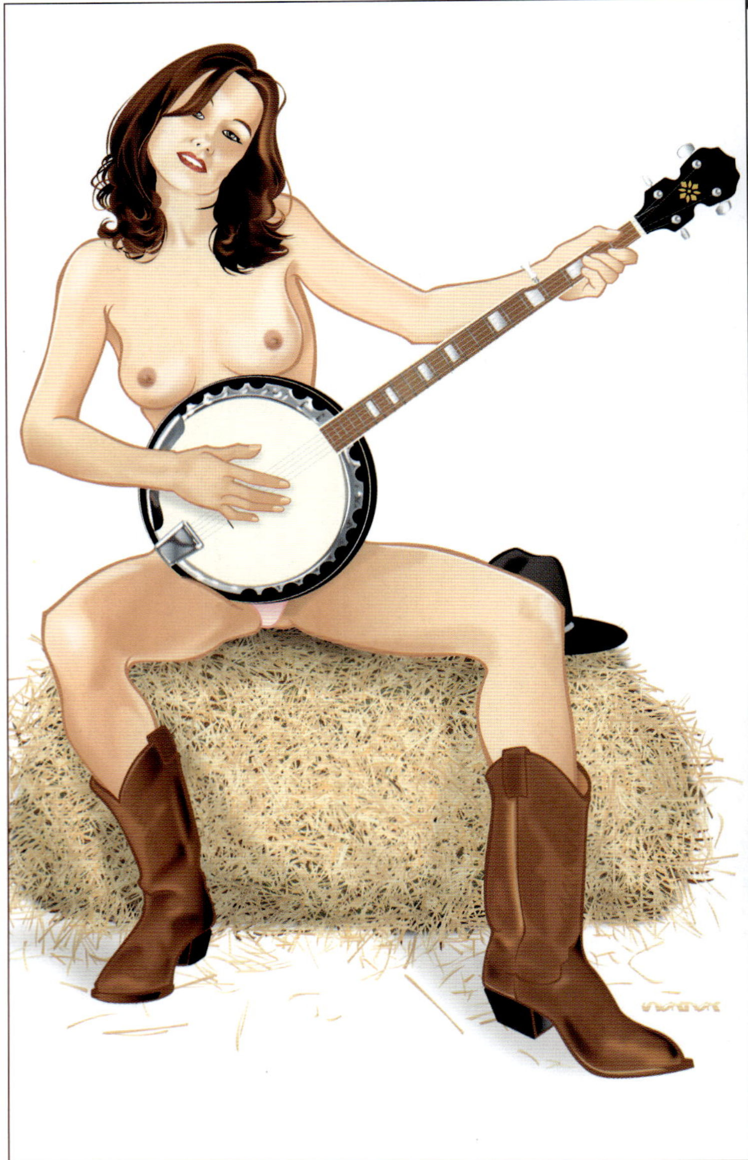

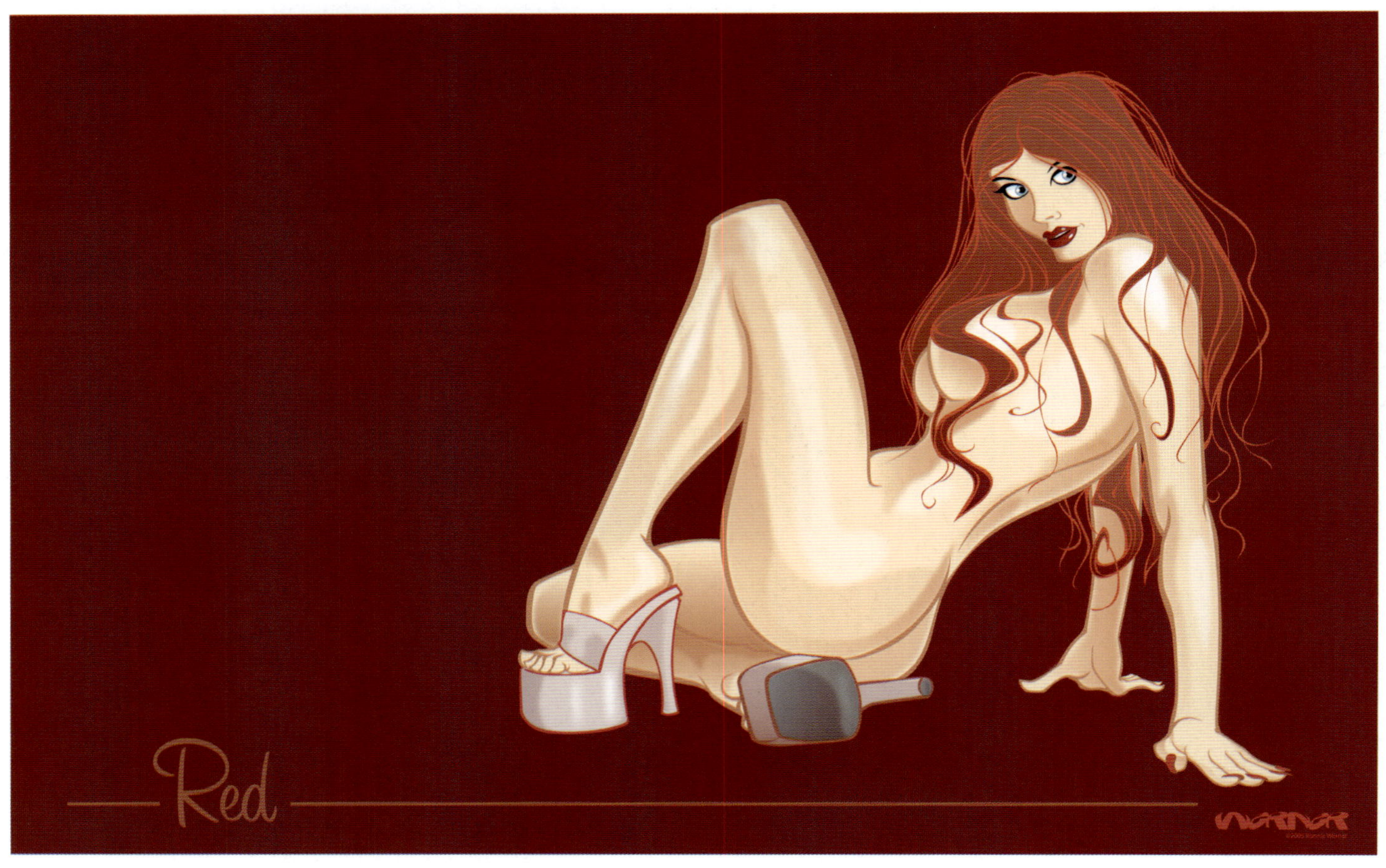
Red

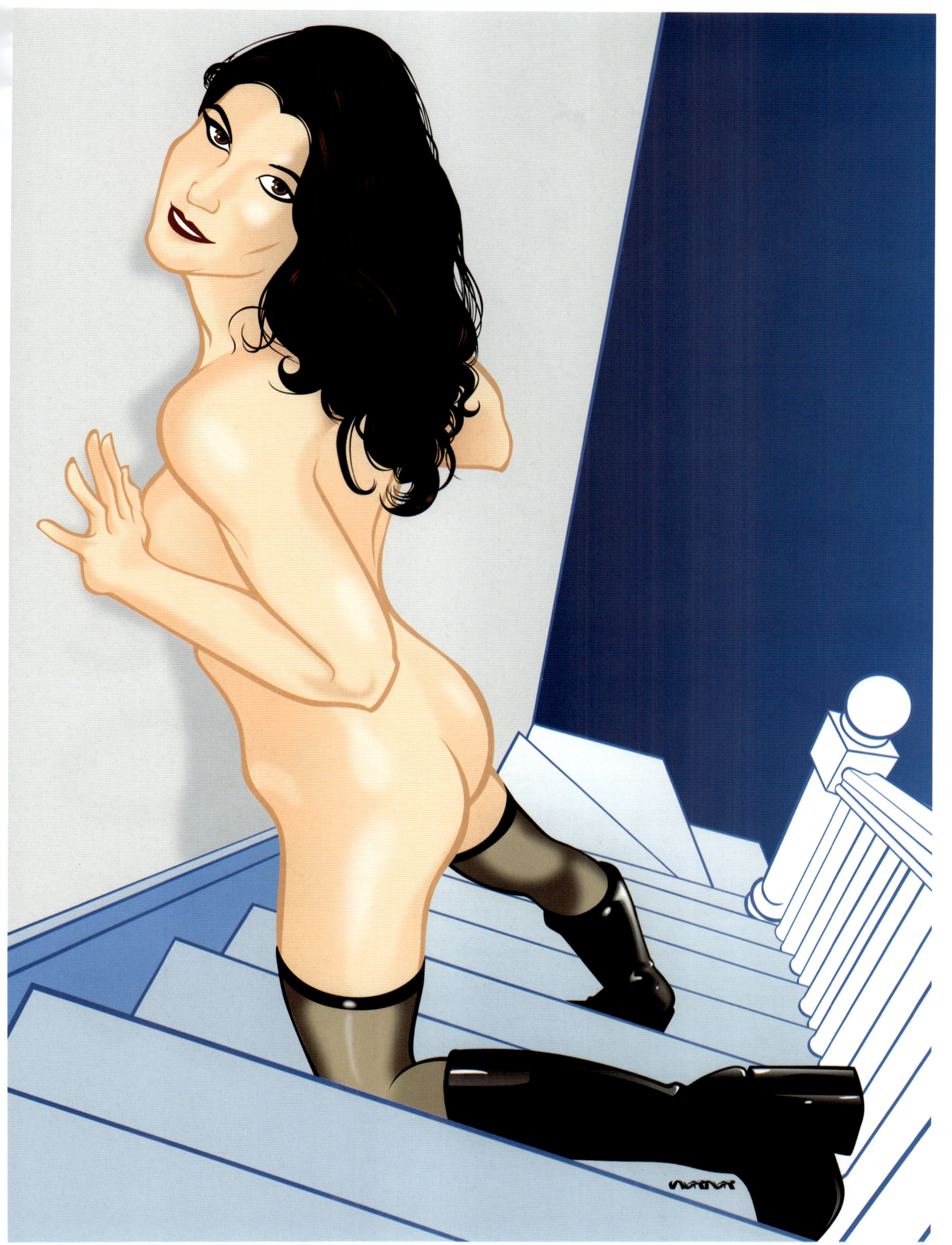

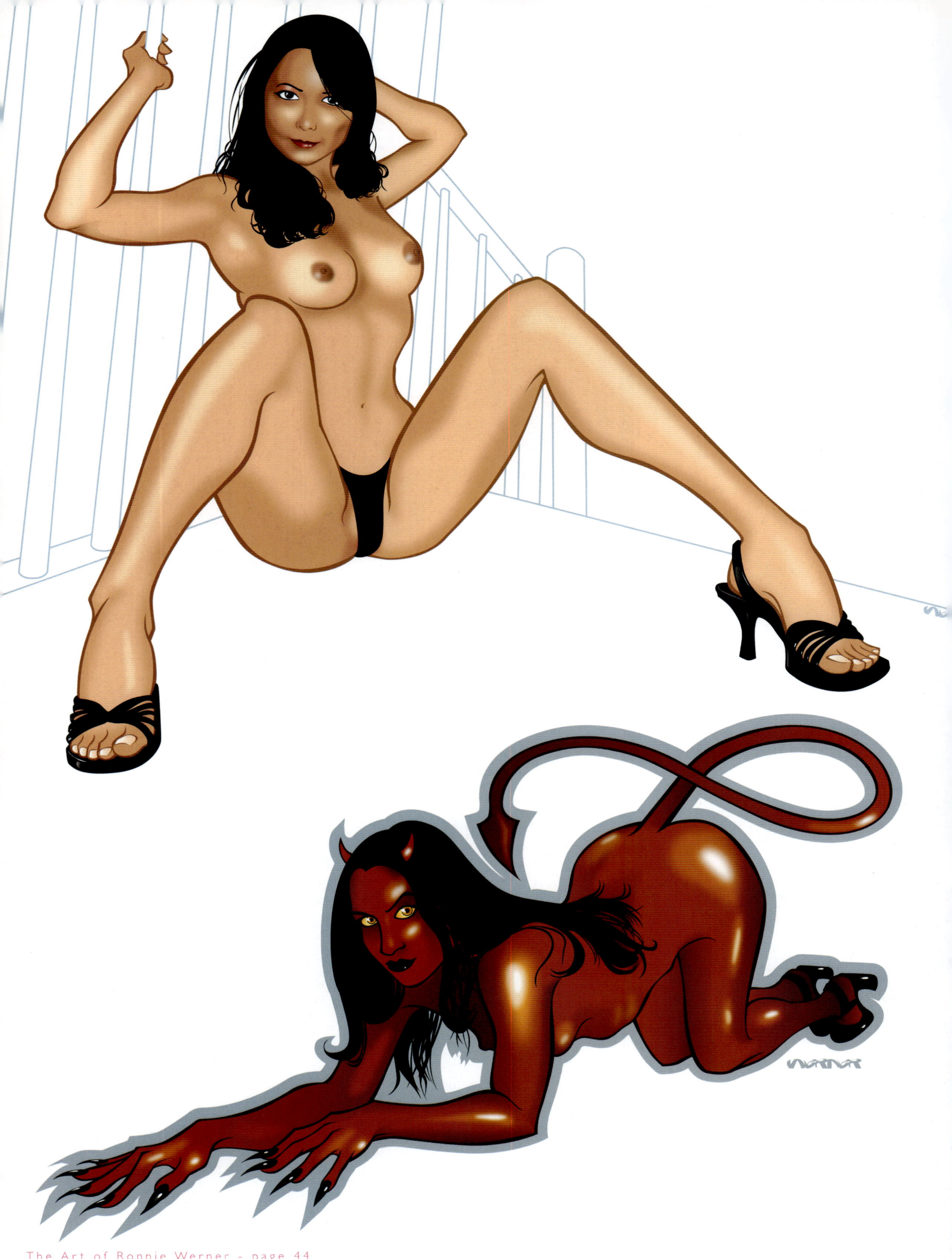

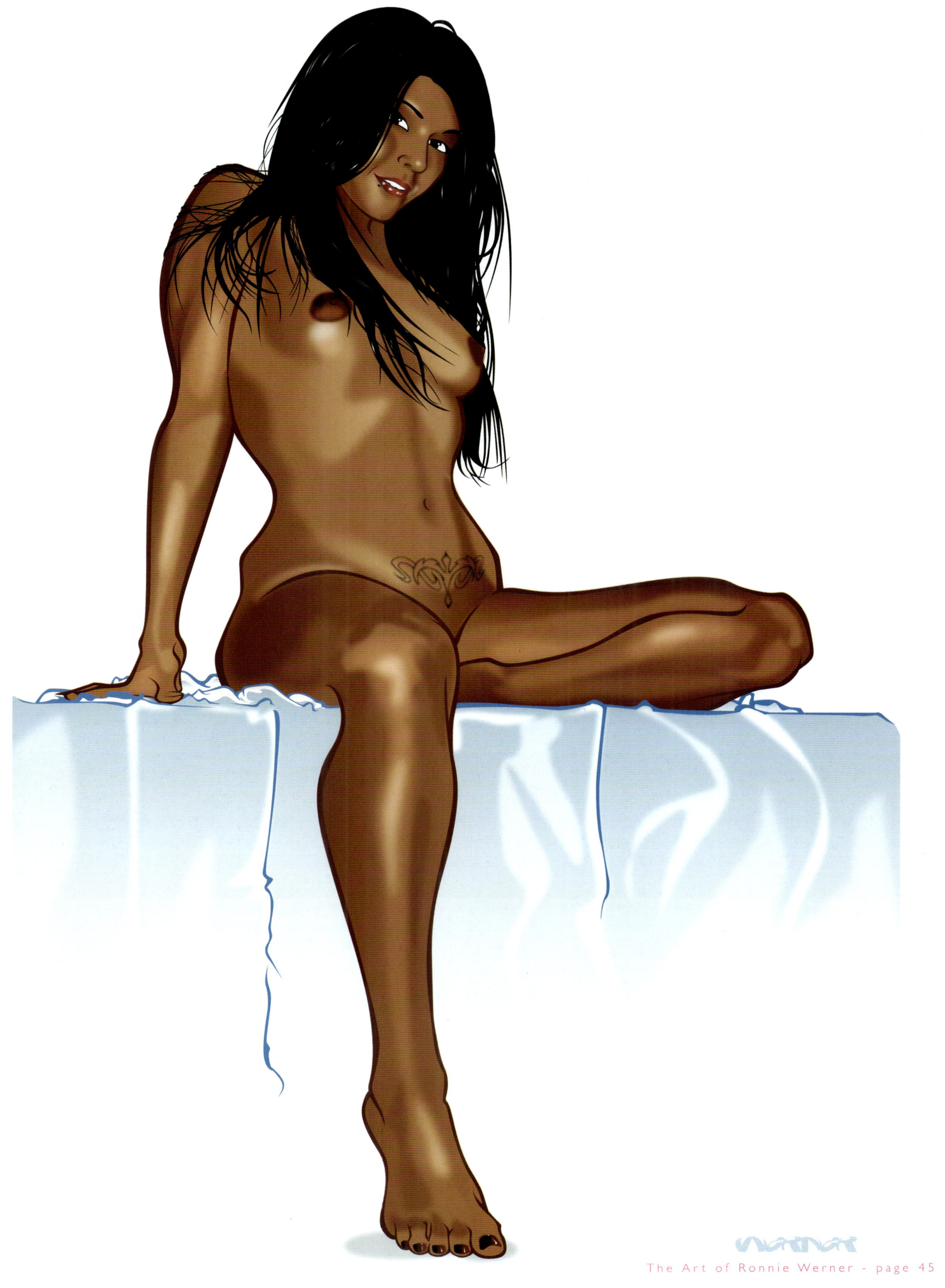

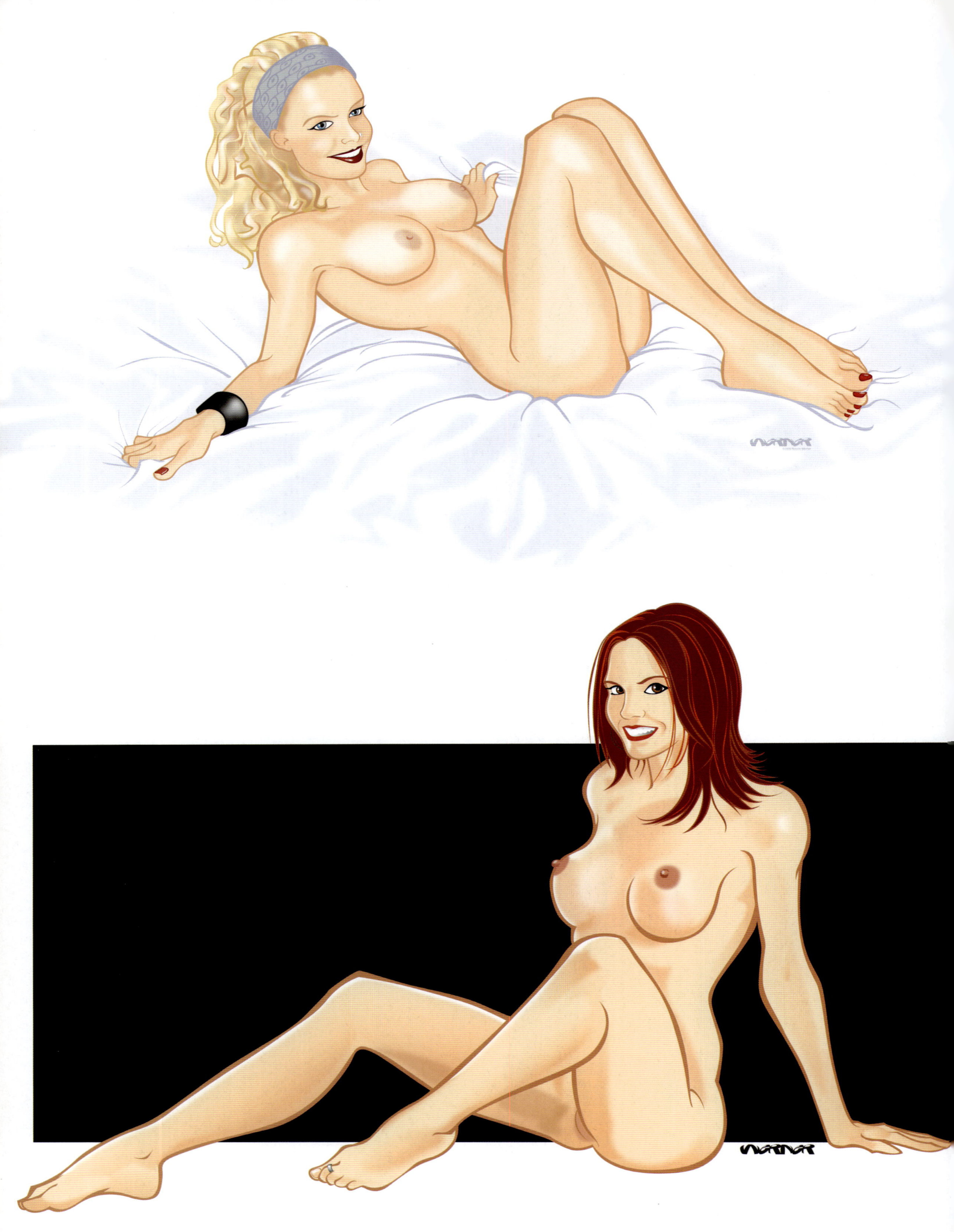

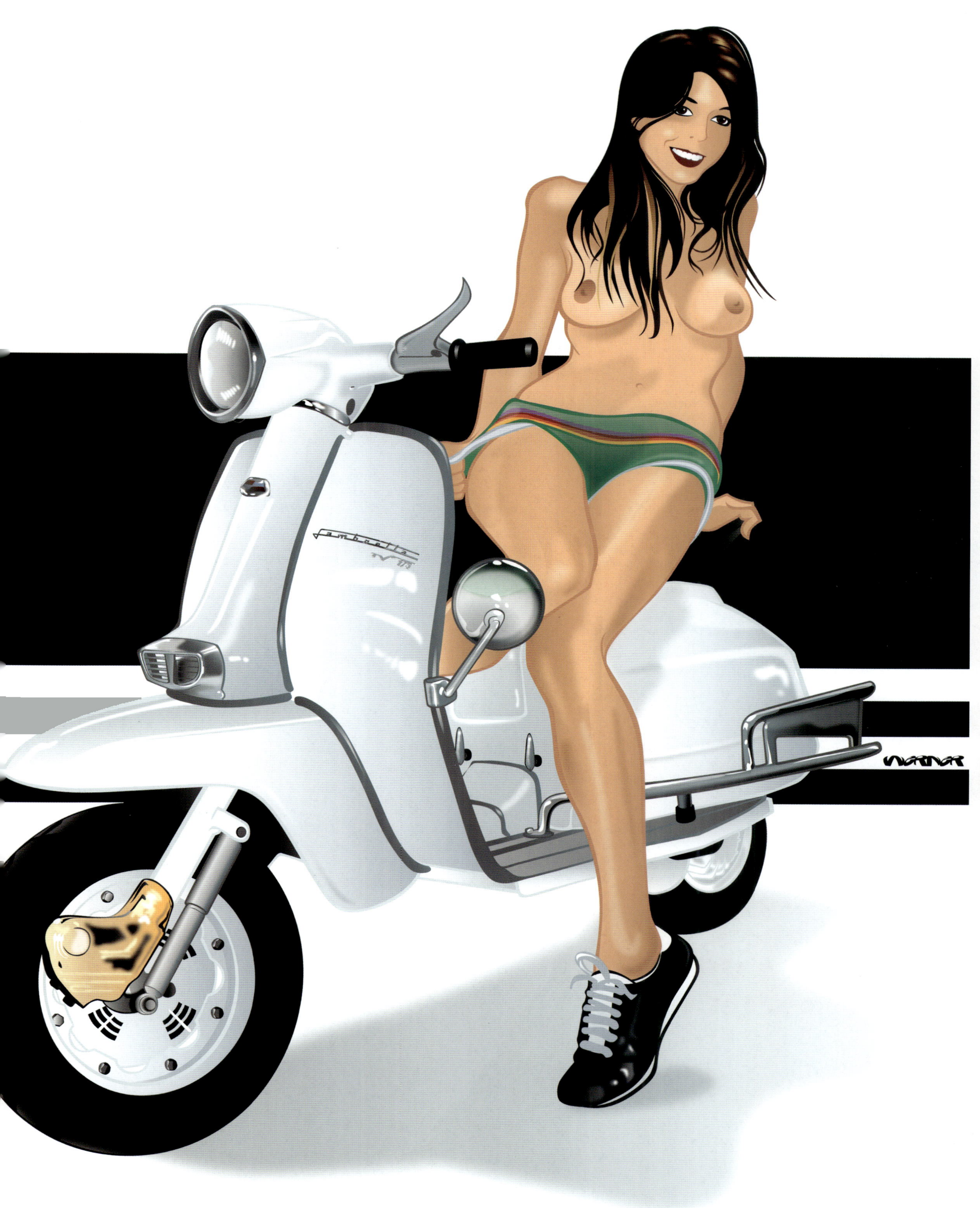
Lambretta
Werner

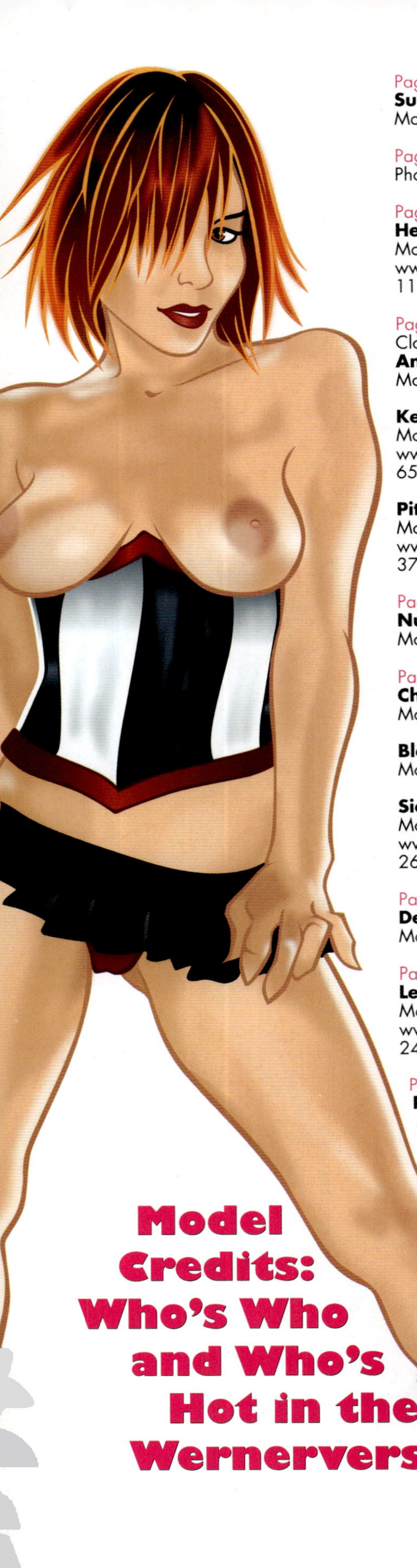

Model Credits: Who's Who and Who's Hot in the Wernerverse

Page 1
Susan
Model: Susan

Page 2
Photo Model: Niki

Page 3
Heather
Model: Heather Feather
www.modelmayhem.com/
11206

Page 4
Clockwise from the top:
Andrea (Red Couch)
Model: Andrea

Kexin
Model: Kexin
www.modelmayhem.com/
65176

Pita Pearl
Model: Violeta Dposey
www.modelmayhem.com/
375172

Page 5
Nursey
Model: Nursey

Page 6
Christina
Model: Christina

Blondie
Model: None

Siobhan
Model: Siobhan W
www.modelmayhem.com/
267132

Page 7
Dena
Model: Dena Dovichi

Page 8
Lemi
Model: Lemi
www.modelmayhem.com/
2438

Page 9
Pistolita
Model: Pistolita Suicide
www.modelmayhem.com/
125079

Page 10
Mirage
Model: Mirage
www.model
mayhem.com/
528468

Page 11
Veronika Bond
Model: Veronika Kotlajic
www.perfectmuse.com
www.GalleryProvocateur.org

Page 12
Clockwise from the top left:
Miss Kel
Model: Miss Kel

Annika
Model: Annika

Amanda
Model: Amanda Stubits
www.modelmayhem.com/
276196

Page 13
Andrea Wings
Model: Andrea

Page 14
Clockwise from the top:
Winged
Model: None

Susan Nude
Model: Susan

Tech Ty
Model: Ty Fyre
www.modelmayhem.com/
356437

Page 15
Veronika Black
Model: Veronika Kotlajic
www.perfectmuse.com
www.GalleryProvocateur.org

Page 16 & 17
Ty Demons
Model: Ty Fyre
www.modelmayhem.com/
356437

Page 18
Cinetique
Model: Cinetique Femme
www.modelmayhem.com/
580279

Page 19
Spacegirl
Model: none

Page 20
Clockwise from the top
Dolphin
Model: none

Carmen
Model: Carmen
www.modelmayhem.com/
carmen

Colleen
Model: Colleen Parker
www.iamween.com

Page 21
Fishnets
Model: none

Page 22
May lu
Model: May lu
www.modelmayhem.com/
51953

Page 23
Cowgirl
Model: none

Page 24 & 25
Clockwise from the top:
Kori
Model: Kori
www.modelmayhem.com/
1044

Andrea
Model: Andrea

Gun Girl
Model: none

Page 26
Violet
Model: Violet

Page 27
Top:
Veronika Fire
Model: Veronika Kotlajic
www.perfectmuse.com
www.GalleryProvocateur.org

Bottom:
Rocket
Model: Rocket
www.modelmayhem.com/
9608

Page 28
Niki and the Snowman
Model: Niki

Page 29
Rakhee Christmas
Model: Rakhee
www.modelmayhem.com/
381817

Page 30
Clockwise from the top left:
Velvet 1
Model: none

Isabelle
Model: Isabelle

Gina
Model: Gina Shannon
www.modelmayhem.com/
19856

Page 31
Velvet 1
Model: none

Page 32
Rakhee
Model: Rakhee
www.modelmayhem.com/
381817

Martina
Model: Miss Martina
www.modelmayhem.com/
3640

Page 33
Veronika
Model: Veronika Kotlajic
www.perfectmuse.com
www.GalleryProvocateur.org

Page 34
Clockwise from the top:
Pita Pearl
Model: Violeta Dposey
www.modelmayhem.com/
375172

Laura
Model: Laura

Robin
Model: Robin

Page 35
Kori Pink
Model: Kori Belle
www.modelmayhem.com,
1044

Page 36
Robin 2
Model: Robin

Page 37
Kexin
Model: Kexin
www.modelmayhem.com,
65176

Page 38
Vitt Vamp
Model: Vittoria
www.vittoriaerotica.com

Page 39
Devi
Model: Devi Dawl
www.modelmayhem.com,
281459

Page 40
Jamie
Model: Jamie

Rocket 2
Model: Rocket
www.modelmayhem.com/
9608

Page 41
Brianne
Model: Brianne
www.modelmayhem.com/
4901

Page 42
Clock wise from the top le
Andrea Red Couch 3
Model: Andrea

Jessi Lu
Model: Jessi Lu
www.modelmayhem.com/
483359

Red
Model: none

Page 43
Annika
Model: Annika

Page 44
Malissa
Model: Malissa

Devil Girl
Model: none

Page 45
Becky
Model: Becky

Page 46
Ingress
Model: ingress

Jen
Model: jusjen
www.modelmayhem.com/
11781

Page 47
Martina Lambretta
Model: Martina Ann
www.modelmayhem.com/
120223

Page 48
Ty Fyre
Model: Ty Fyre
www.modelmayhem.com/
356437